English for the construction industry

Graham and Celia Waterhouse

MACMILLAN
PUBLISHERS

First published 1981
Reprinted 1984, 1985, 1988, 1991, 1994.

Published by *Macmillan Publishers Ltd*
London and Basingstoke

A tape is available to accompany this book

Acknowledgements
The authors would like to thank James Cumming for his invaluable
contribution to the planning of this book, and for his suggestions and
encouragement thereafter, and Sue Dickerson for typing the manuscript.

ISBN 0-333-31254-6

Printed in Malaysia

The Cavendish Hotel mentioned in Unit 9 is purely fictional and bears
no relation to any hotel of that name.

Contents

Unit Four   Cladding, Glazing and Scaffolding

Unit Five   Carpentry and Joinery

Unit Six   Finishes

Unit Seven   Plumbing and Drainage

Unit Eight   Heating, Ventilation and Electrical Services

Unit Nine   External Works and Landscaping

Introduction

Guidelines to help students using this book

Unit Zero is a reference unit. It introduces the people who work on a typical building project, to help you understand the jobs of the people you meet in the book, or in real life on site. It also introduces the names of the drawings and written documents you may have to read when you are working on a building site. You may need to refer to this Unit while you are working on other Units of the book.

Units One to Nine are written around the construction of a building from foundations (Unit One) to landscaping (Unit Nine). Each Unit is designed to stand by itself. The language and reference material is at the same level in each Unit, so you do not have to work through the book in order. You can start with whichever Unit is most useful for you, from the point of view of either language material or reference material.

Each Unit is in three main parts:
Language Practice
Communication on Site
Reference Section

Language Practice

Each of the three sections can be used on its own, or you can work through them all together starting with whichever you wish. Work through each section like this.

a Read through the conversation. Check up all the Reference Section words you don't know, and make sure you understand all the words and know who all the people are (see 0.1).
If you have the tape, listen to the conversation several times. Read the conversation aloud. This will be useful for your English even if you are studying on your own, because all the conversations use everyday spoken English. If you have the tape, try to copy the intonation of the speakers.
When you are familiar with the conversation and understand what is happening, do the exercises. If you do them without looking back at the conversation, it will be a good test of your understanding.
b It is a good idea to work through all of **a** before you start **b** but at least make sure you understand the conversation and know who the speakers are before you try the exercise in **b**.

Communication on Site

This section develops language material from the three conversations in the Language Practice. Many of the exercises are based on situations in the conversations, so before you start you should be familiar with all three conversations from the Unit. You should work through Communication on Site in order.

Reference Section

This section is intended to help you understand all kinds of building words which you might hear or wish to use in conversations and discussions on site, or which you might see on a drawing or in a specification. In each Unit the words have been sorted into various groups. This will help you to use the Reference Section as a learning tool to build up your vocabulary of building words, and is also a convenient way of reminding you of the names of materials and tools you are using. The different groups in the Reference Section are:

Materials

'Building materials' usually means goods which are delivered to a building site to be made into a building. In the Reference Sections, however, a material generally means a substance which has not been through a manufacturing process to be made into an object or 'thing' of some sort. (Such manufactured objects, eg bricks, have been listed as components.)

Components

These are objects or parts which have been made from one or more materials. Some examples are metal sheets, window frames.

Where lists of materials and components are only short they have been grouped together.

Tools and plant or accessories

Tools are objects which are used to work on materials and components and help fix them all together; plant is large machinery for doing various jobs and for manufacturing; accessories are useful items necessary for certain jobs, which cannot be classed as either tools or plant.

Actions

These words are verbs which building tradesmen use to describe what jobs they do on site. Many of them seem obvious, but you may find it useful to check that the words you use to describe your own job are correct.

General

These are important words which do not fit into any other group, such as the names of parts of buildings or components, new words invented by builders (jargon) and abstract concepts.

Drawings and Specifications

Here you can find words specifically associated with drawn information and written specifications, and lists of symbols used on architectural drawings are included where appropriate.

List of Abbreviations

A	amp
Abs.	asbestos
Abs.ct.	asbestos cement
A.C.	alternate current
al.	aluminium
B.G.	Birmingham gauge (for metal thicknesses)
bit.	bitumen
bldg.	building
B.M.	bench mark
B.S.P.T.	British Standard Pipe Thread
bwk.	brickwork
C.I.	cast iron
col.	column
conc.	concrete
C.P.	chromium plate
cpd.	cupboard
D.C.	direct current
D.P.C.	damp proof course
D.P.M.	damp proof membrane
dwg.	drawing
E.L.C.B.	earth leakage circuit-breaker
E.M.L.	expanded metal lathing
eg	for example
ex.	out of (eg a length of timber which has been planed from a length of size 75 × 38mm can be described as ex. 75 × 38)
F.A.I.	fresh air inlet
F.F.L.	finished floor level
fin.	finished (size)
G.L.	ground level
grano	granolithic
G.R.C.	glass reinforced cement
G.R.P.	glass reinforced plastic
H.P.H.W.	high pressure hot water
h.w.	hardwood
ie	that is
I.E.E.	Institution of Electrical Engineers
inv.	invert level

kW.	kilowatt
L.P.H.W.	low pressure hot water
m	metre
M.C.B.	miniature circuit breaker
M.I.C.C.	mineral insulated copper covered
mm	millimetre(s)
M.P.H.W.	medium pressure hot water
M.S.	mild steel
O.Q.	ordinary quality
perpend.	perpendicular joint (in brickwork)
P.F.	pitch fibre
P.F.A.	pulverised fuel ash
P.M.E.	primary mains earthing
P.V.A.	polyvinyl acetate
P.V.C.	polyvinyl chloride
rad.	radiator
R.C.	reinforced concrete
R.S.C.	rolled steel channel
R.S.J.	rolled steel joist
R.W.H.	rainwater head
R.W.P.	rainwater pipe
S.A.A.	satin anodised aluminium
S.C.	satin chrome
S.Q.	selected quality
S.S.	stainless steel
S.V.P.	soil and vent pipe
s.w.	softwood
S.W.G.	standard wire gauge (for metal thicknesses)
T.B.M.	temporary bench mark
t. & g.	tongue and groove
U.B.	universal beam
V.	volt
W.	watt
w.c.	water closet
W.B.P.	weather and boil proof
w.h.b.	wash hand basin

CI/SFB References   CI/SFB is an international system for classifying all kinds of information used in the building industry. The system, which uses combinations of numbers and letters (eg (21.6)H), is used to classify product information and technical libraries, and has been found useful as a way of classifying large sets of production information used on site in constructing buildings.

Where appropriate CI/SFB references have been given for words in the Reference Sections immediately after the word itself.

Unit Zero

0.1 People who work on site

brickie bricklayer (short word)
bricklayer building tradesman who lays bricks
buyer person who buys materials
carpenter building tradesman who works with wood
chief foreman general foreman
chippie carpenter (short word) .
clerk of works person employed by the client, who makes daily checks on the quality of site work
electrician building tradesman who installs electrical wiring and fittings
foreman person who supervises other tradesmen, eg foreman scaffolder; foreman plumber
gang group of people who work together, eg gang of bricklayers
ganger person who works in a gang
general foreman person who supervises several other foremen
groundworker site workman
joiner craftsman who makes components out of wood
labourer workman who helps with many kinds of work, often carrying materials
mate person who helps a skilled tradesman, eg electrician's mate
pair two tradesmen who work together, eg pair of bricklayers
plasterer building tradesman who works with plaster and other finishes
plumber building tradesman who works with pipework and flashings
quantity surveyor person who measures and records work done on site
resident architect architect who has an office on a very large site
resident engineer consultant engineer who has an office on a very large site
scaffolder person who erects scaffolding
site agent building contractor's representative in charge of a site
site engineer person who does setting out and other technical work on site, including supervision
spark electrician (short word)
steelfixer person who fixes steel bars for reinforced concrete
tiler person who fixes roof tiles
tradesman skilled building workman

0.2.a Drawings

assembly drawing detail drawing showing how part of a building is put together, see fig. 0

component drawing drawing of a part of a building, eg a window

detail section see fig. 0

elevation see fig. 0

floor plan plan of one floor of a building

location drawing plan showing where parts and components of a building are located

perspective drawing see fig. 0

plan see fig. 0

plan detail see fig. 0

production drawing working drawing

section see fig. 0

site layout site plan

site plan plan showing position of buildings and other parts of a site

survey drawing plan of a site before building starts, showing existing features and levels

working drawing drawing used to build a building

0.2.b Documents

bill of quantities list of materials and work required to build a building

daywork sheet record sheet for work done which is in addition to the contract work

form of contract list of terms and conditions which apply to a contract between a client and a contractor

insurance policy document which lists the terms and conditions of an insurance contract

insurance premium sum of money paid for insurance cover, so that damage caused to a building would be paid for by the insurance company

licence official permit

programme chart which shows the time in which a contractor intends to build a building

schedule list of building components, eg door schedule; schedule of sanitary ware

site minutes written record of a site meeting

soil report information prepared by an engineer about site ground conditions

specification written description of work to be done

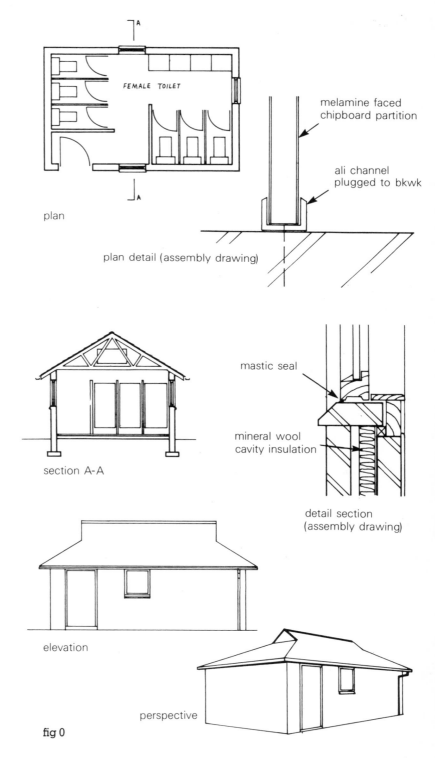

FEMALE TOILET

plan

plan detail (assembly drawing)

melamine faced
chipboard partition

ali channel
plugged to bkwk

section A-A

mastic seal

mineral wool
cavity insulation

detail section
(assembly drawing)

elevation

perspective

fig 0

3

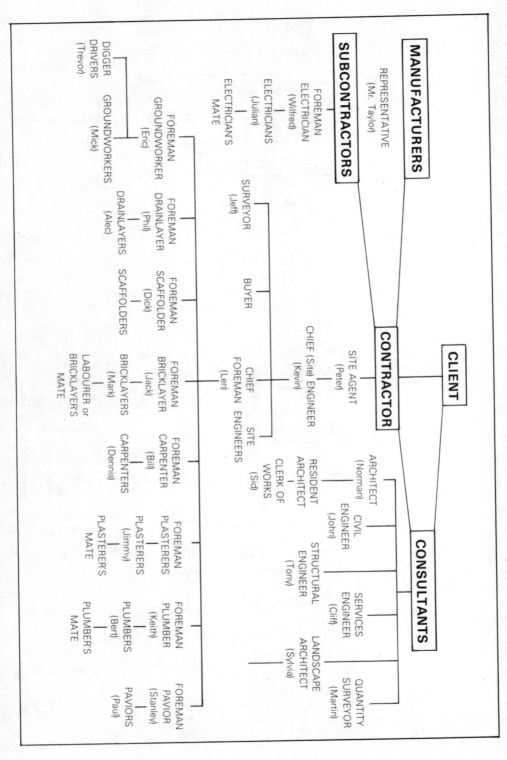

MANUFACTURERS

REPRESENTATIVE
(Mr. Taylor)

SUBCONTRACTORS

FOREMAN
ELECTRICIAN
(Wilfred)

ELECTRICIANS
(Julian)

ELECTRICIAN'S
MATE

DIGGER
DRIVERS
(Trevor).

GROUNDWORKERS
(Mick)

FOREMAN
GROUNDWORKER
(Eric)

DRAINLAYERS
(Alec)

FOREMAN
DRAINLAYER
(Phil)

SCAFFOLDERS

FOREMAN
SCAFFOLDER
(Dick)

SURVEYOR
(Jeff)

BUYER

BRICKLAYERS
(Jack)

FOREMAN
BRICKLAYER
(Len)

LABOURER or
BRICKLAYER'S
MATE

CHIEF
FOREMAN

CLIENT

CONTRACTOR

SITE AGENT
(Peter)

CHIEF (Site) ENGINEER
(Kevin)

CHIEF
FOREMAN

SITE
ENGINEERS

CLERK OF
WORKS
(Sid)

CONSULTANTS

ARCHITECT
(Norman)

RESIDENT
ARCHITECT

CARPENTERS
(Dennis)

FOREMAN
CARPENTER
(Bill)

CIVIL
ENGINEER
(John)

STRUCTURAL
ENGINEER
(Tony)

PLASTERERS
(Jimmy)

FOREMAN
PLASTERERS

PLASTERER'S
MATE

SERVICES
ENGINEER
(Cliff)

PLUMBERS
(Bert)

FOREMAN
PLUMBER
(Keith)

PLUMBER'S
MATE

LANDSCAPE
ARCHITECT
(Sylvia)

QUANTITY
SURVEYOR
(Martin)

PAVIORS
(Paul)

FOREMAN
PAVIOR
(Stanley)

1 Site Establishment, Setting Out and Substructure

Language Practice

1.1.a Site Planning

'How to build on a crowded site'
The first thing a contractor looks for on a site plan is working space. If there is not enough room in which to work, he may have to think carefully about which buildings should be constructed first.

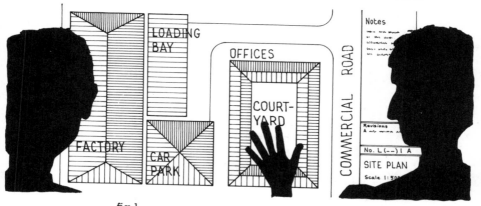

fig 1

Peter – *Site Agent*   Kevin – *Site Engineer*

Peter Just look at this site plan, Kevin. We're going to have problems here, you know.

Kevin Hmm – yes, I can see that. There isn't really enough room to work, is there?

Peter Well, no. I can't see where we'll be able to stockpile topsoil, for a start.

Kevin No. And I don't know where we're going to put our site offices either . . . Well, perhaps we could try putting them inside the courtyard. Do you think it's big enough?

Peter Well, let's see . . . how much space is there? . . . Hmm, only about a hundred square metres. Well, that won't be big enough, will it?

Kevin Well, no . . . but I suppose we could always use a scaffold platform and have two-storey offices.

Peter Oh no, they're so inconvenient. And anyway, the huts would be in the way there, really. But listen, we can do it another way, I think. The factory's the least accessible building, isn't it?

Kevin Yes, I think so.

Peter Then it would be a good idea to set that out first. We could get the groundslab in there quickly, couldn't we?

Kevin Oh yes. And we could put the site huts up there while all the other foundations are being laid.

Peter That's right. And after that I suggest we get on with the office block straight away. If we get the offices watertight as soon as possible, we'll be able to use them as our own offices, you see. Won't we?

accessible able to be reached
block building
construct build
contractor *see* 0.1
courtyard *see* 9.5.b
crowded with not much room left over
foundations *see* 1.9.e
groundslab *see* fig. 11 **concrete groundslab**
hut *see* 1.5
inconvenient difficult to use
platform flat, raised area

scaffold *see* 4.7
set out *see* 1.7.b
site office *see* 1.5
site plan *see* 0.2
space room
stockpile store for future use
storey one floor or level of a building, eg a ten-storey building is a building with ten floors
topsoil *see* 1.8.b
watertight able to keep out water

Answer the questions.
1 What problems does Kevin see on the site plan?
2 Why can't they put the offices in the courtyard?
3 What does Kevin suggest using a scaffold platform for?
4 What does Peter think of two-storey offices?
5 Where do they decide to put the huts up? How will they manage this?
6 What will they use as their own offices when building has started?

Complete the sentences.
1 We shan't even be able to stockpile topsoil because . . . . . .
2 The courtyard's only about a hundred square metres, so . . . . . .
3 The courtyard's no good for siting offices anyway because . . . . . .
4 It's best to set the factory out first because . . . . . .
5 If we get the groundslab in quickly in the factory, then . . . . . .
6 We shan't be able to use the office buildings as our own offices until . . . . . .

1.1.b Tag questions Look at these sentences from the conversation:
There isn't really enough room to work, *is there?*
That won't be big enough, *will it?*
The factory's the least accessible building, *isn't it?*
Tag questions at the end of sentences are used a lot in conversation. Notice that 'not' (or 'n't') comes *either* in the main part of the sentence

or in the tag question, but not in both. Practise using tag questions in this exercise:

Example:
We'd better have two-storey offices here, ... ?
We'd better have two-storey offices here, *hadn't we?*

1 You could use a scaffold platform, ... ?
2 They should make the offices watertight as soon as possible, ... ?
3 The contractor won't start building before December, ... ?
4 The huts would be in the way there, ... ?
5 They're not laying the foundations yet, ... ?
6 We've got problems here, ... ?

1.2.a Excavation

'Unearthing a surprise'

If excavations for foundations unexpectedly show difficult soil conditions, the structural engineer has to decide quickly what should be done.

fig 2

Tony – *Structural Engineer*   Peter – *Site Agent*

Tony Hmm, yes, I see the problem. We didn't expect to find sand here, did we? Well, we'll certainly have to do something about it. There are supposed to be strip footings here, I think, aren't there?
Peter Yes, that's right.
Tony Well, I'm afraid it won't be much good if we just leave it. That sand could easily give way under the foundations.
Peter Yes, that's just what I thought. There'll be four storeys going here, you know, so it'll be taking a fair load.
Tony Yes. And you say you've excavated the trench to the usual depth of one metre? So how far down did you come across this sand, then?
Peter Oh, it must have been about 500 millimetres down when we first saw it.
Tony I see. Okay. Well, first I think you ought to excavate another 450 millimetres to see whether you can get through it.

7

Peter Right you are.

Tony If you do manage to, then you can backfill with leanmix concrete before you pour your foundations.

Peter Okay. And what if we don't get through it? Don't you think we should have a wider footing or something?

Tony Yes, if the outcrop is still there, then obviously I'll have to redesign that footing. You'll have to make it wider, and put in some reinforcement as well, I should think. Er – I'd better have a drawing ready for you tomorrow in case it's needed.

backfill *see* 1.8.b
excavation *see* 1.8
fair considerable
foundation *see* 1.9.e
leanmix concrete *see* 1.9.b
load weight
manage be able
obviously clearly
outcrop layer
redesign draw up again

reinforcement *see* 2.6.a **steel reinforcement bar**
sand *see* 1.9.a **aggregate**
soil *see* fig. 8
storey one floor or level of a building, eg a ten-storey building is a building with ten floors.
strip footing *see* 1.9.e
trench *see* fig. 8
unearth dig up

Answer the questions.

1 Why does the structural engineer think something will have to be done about the problem?

2 How high will the building be when it is finished?

3 What is the usual depth of excavations? At what depth did they first see the sand?

4 Why does Tony want another 450mm excavated?

5 What will they do if they manage to get through the sand?

6 What will Tony do in case they don't get through the sand?

Fill in the blanks to complete Peter's report on the morning's work on site.

This morning we started . . . . . . At approximately 500mm depth we . . . . . . This was very unexpected and the structural engineer thinks . . . . . . He says we must . . . . . . If we manage to get through the sand, he wants us to . . . . . . But if there's still an outcrop of sand at 1,450mm, then . . . . . .

1.2.b 'If' clauses (present tense)

Look at these sentences from the conversation:

It won't be much good *if we just leave it*.

If you do manage to, then you can backfill with leanmix concrete.

If the outcrop is still there, . . . I'll have to redesign that footing.

All these sentences are conditional sentences using 'if'. Each sentence is in two parts or clauses: one 'if' clause (in *italics*) and one main clause. When we have the present tense in the 'if' clause, we can use present or future in the main clause. (We don't use the future in the 'if' clause itself). Do the following exercise to practise using 'if' sentences. Join each pair of sentences to make one 'if' sentence.

Example:
The excavator finds an outcrop of sand.
Peter has to report it to the structural engineer.
If the excavator finds an outcrop of sand, Peter has to report it to the structural engineer.

1 We reinforce the foundations.
There won't be any problems.
2 It's hard to dig the foundations.
The subsoil contains rock.
3 The foundations will possibly give way.
We don't make the footings wider.
4 The excavator gets through the layer of sand.
They are going to backfill with leanmix concrete.
5 You make the footing wider.
The foundations will be firm enough.
6 You can wait till tomorrow.
I'll have the drawing ready for you.

1.3.a Concreting

'A clerk of works is never satisfied'
The clerk of works is responsible to the client and his architect to ensure that all work on site is carried out properly. He cannot afford to overlook the smallest defect.

fig 3

Sid – *Clerk of Works*   Kevin – *Site Engineer*   (Mick – *Groundworker*)

Sid Oh, Kevin, I'm glad I've caught you. Peter asked me to approve the reinforcement for this raft as soon as it's ready.

Kevin Oh, they've just finished. They're going to pour the concrete first thing tomorrow.

Sid I know. But look here, Kevin, you haven't got enough spacer blocks to keep the steel off the bottom, you know.

9

Kevin Oh . . . well, we put them in at three metre centres. I thought that would be enough with this heavy steel mesh.

Sid But look, you can see for yourself – the steel's sagging so much you're not even going to have as much as 38 millimetres' cover to it in some places. We can't have that, now, can we?

Kevin Oh dear, I didn't realise it was so bad. Do you think we should put more spacers in, then?

Sid Hmm . . . well, perhaps you should just try turning these blocks on end first and see if that would raise the mesh a few more millimetres. That might just do it, you know.

Kevin Okay, we'll give it a try, then.

Sid Right. And the other thing is – I advised you to clear that spoil right away. Just look at it now. It's got pushed right back over the edge in some places. You can't pour concrete on to a bottom like that. It's not good enough.

Kevin Oh yes, I *do* know about that. Mick's going to clear it before he goes home.

Sid All right, he'd better. And give me a call when it's done, and then I can get off home too. I'm going to check over the rest of the site now.

approve accept	**raft** *see* 1.9.e **raft foundation**
bottom base of an excavation	**reinforcement** *see* 2.6.a **steel**
clear remove	**reinforcement**
concrete *see* 1.9.b	**sagging** sinking in the middle
cover *see* 2.6.d	**spacer block** *see* 2.6.a
defect fault	**spoil** *see* 1.8.b
properly correctly	**steel mesh** *see* 2.6.a

Answer the questions.
1 Who has to approve the reinforcement for the concrete raft?
2 Why does Sid think there aren't enough spacer blocks?
3 Why will Kevin turn the blocks on end?
4 What has happened to some of the spoil?
5 Where should the spoil be?
6 What is Mick going to do?

Fill in the blanks.
Sid does not approve the steel reinforcement because . . . . There won't be 38 mm cover to the steel in places because . . . . But they can raise the mesh by . . . . . . Sid also says they won't be able to pour concrete until . . . . Sid won't be going home until . . . . . .

1.3.b 'To be going to'

'To be going to' can express intention or prediction. Look at these sentences:

We're going to put in spacer blocks as soon as possible.
Sid's going to come down and check it over.

'To be going to' here expresses *intention* to do something in the future. It can also express a *prediction* of something which will happen in the future, as these next sentences show:

10

We're not going to get this finished on time.
He's going to find out he hasn't got enough spacers.
Using 'going to' instead of an ordinary future tense gives your words more force as either a prediction or an intention. It can therefore add strength to what you are saying.

Look through the conversation again and find the places where 'going to' is used. Practise using it yourself in this exercise. Each time, change the future tense to 'going to'.

Example:
This mesh is sagging too much. (We'll put in more spacers.)
We're going to put in more spacers.

---

1 Sid's coming down to the site. (He'll check over the reinforcement)
2 Some of the spoil has got pushed right back.
(Sid won't let us pour the concrete until it's been cleared)
3 Sid's going to look at the reinforcement mesh. (He won't be very pleased with it)
4 Kevin hasn't put in enough spacers. (He'll not have enough cover to the steel)
5 There's a lot of spoil near the edges. (They'll have to clear it before they go home)
6 Sid is checking over the site. (Kevin will give him a call when the spoil has been cleared)

Communication on Site

Making suggestions and giving advice

1.4.a Making suggestions

It is useful to know how to make suggestions on site, where we might have to help someone to find the best way of coping with a problem, or where we might see a better way of doing something. Here are some ways we make suggestions:

You can/could maybe . . . . . .
Can't/couldn't we perhaps . . . . . ?
How about . . . . . ?
It would be a good idea if . . . . . .
We can/could always . . . . . .
Let's try . . . . . .
Why not try . . . . . ?
I suggest . . . . . .
I was thinking of . . . . . .

Look at conversation 1.1.a where Peter and Kevin are trying to find a space for the site offices. What suggestions do they make to each other? Now you practise making suggestions to cope with all the following problems. Use a different expression for each problem.
1 The courtyard isn't big enough for the site huts.
2 There seems to be nowhere on site to stockpile topsoil.
3 The excavator has unexpectedly struck a layer of sand at 700 mm.
4 There is still sand at a depth of 1,200 mm.

5 The steel reinforcement mesh is sagging too much.

6 Kevin has turned the spacers on end and there is still not enough cover to the steel.

1.4.b Polite suggestions

On site we often have to talk to different people doing many different jobs. Each job has a different rank, or level of importance. For example, Peter, the site agent, has a higher job rank than Mick, the groundworker. Trevor, the digger driver, has a lower job rank than Sid, the clerk of works.

In conversation we often talk in a different way to people of different job rank. We do this when we make suggestions. To people of lower rank we can be quite direct about making suggestions, but to people of higher job rank we are usually more polite. Things we might say are:

Perhaps it might be a good idea if . . . . . .

I hope you don't mind me suggesting this, but couldn't we . . . . . ?

Do you think perhaps we could try . . . . . ?

I thought it might be possible to . . . . . .

Now make some suggestions to someone of higher job rank about:

1 Strengthening the foundations in an unexpected outcrop of sand.

2 Checking security on site after some equipment has been stolen.

3 Using two-storey offices because there isn't enough room on site for one-storey ones.

1.4.c Giving advice

When we make suggestions we are putting forward our own ideas on the best way to do things. Sometimes on site we may be asked for our advice on what to do. Advice is often based on our own experience or knowledge. When we advise somebody, we usually have more experience of the thing he is doing than he has himself. Here are some ways we can give advice:

I think you ought to . . . . . .

Don't you think you should . . . . . ?

You'd better . . . . . .

You'll have to . . . . . .

You really ought to . . . . . , you know.

Shouldn't you try . . . . . ?

I'd advise you to . . . . . .

If I were you, I'd . . . . . .

Tony gives some advice to Peter in conversation 1.2.a How does he do this? Look back to exercise 1.4.a and this time give your advice on what to do in each of the problem situations.

1.4.d Practice conversations

Now practise writing your own conversations making suggestions and giving advice.

Words you will need:

demolition *see* 1.6

brick *see* 2.5.a

tip *see* 1.8.b

waterproof able to keep out water

1 You are Andy, a demolition labourer. You are talking to Len, the chief foreman. The building you are demolishing is coming down

easily and you don't think you'll need the demolition equipment which has been ordered. Also, you think some of the old bricks are good enough to sell instead of sending them to the tip. Write your conversation with Len, making suggestions to him and giving him your advice. (You do all the talking; he says only 'Oh yes?', 'Why?', 'Do you think so?' and so on.)

Begin like this:

Andy: *Could I just have a word with you, Len? You see . . . . . .*

2 You are Eric, the foreman groundworker. You are talking to Trevor, the digger driver. He has begun excavating trenches and wants to get finished by the end of the day. You think he ought to stop because it looks like rain and you are worried about the trenches getting filled with water. There are a lot of things he could help with instead (such as covering the trenches with good waterproof covering, clearing away the spoil from the edges, putting equipment away in the store, etc). Write your conversation with Trevor, making suggestions and giving advice. (You do all the talking as before; he says only 'Oh', 'Yes', 'Okay', and so on.)

Begin like this:

Eric: *Hey, Trevor, you're not going to go on with the excavating now, are you? . . . . .*

Reference Section

1.5 Site Establishment

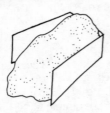

bunker

fence

access way of getting into a site
bunker open area to contain sand or aggregates
canteen room in which meals are served
drinking water water clean enough to drink
drying room room in which wet clothes may be dried
first-aid kit box or store containing plasters, bandages, and simple medicines in case of accidents on site
helmet (B7c) hard protective hat
hoarding high fence to protect a site
hut small building used on site, which is taken away afterwards
latrine toilet building used by people working on a building site
plant (B) machines and equipment
portable building building which may be moved complete on a lorry
portable track (B2) strong sheet material laid down to make a road over soft ground
production information (A3) all drawings, specifications and schedules required to construct a building
security protection of materials from thieves
set of drawings (A3t) the drawings required to construct a building
shed small building, usually used as a store
site boundary line around the edge of the site
site office site agent's office
staging platform on which to put site offices above the ground
stand pipe temporary water supply point
statutory authority authority providing services, such as water, gas or electricity
stretcher device on which to carry an injured man to first-aid room
washing facilities hot and cold water supply for workmen to wash themselves
watching and lighting provision of lights and night guard for security reasons

first-aid kit

helmet

stand pipe

1.6 Demolition (D2) and Shoring (B2)

bitch   dog

adjustable steel prop (B2d) see fig. 4
ball and chain (B2b) demolition device; see fig. 4
bitch t6 simple steel fastener used in timber shoring
breaker (B2b) tool for breaking up concrete
compressor (B8f) machine providing air for power tools
dead shore (B2d) see fig. 4
demolish (D2) knock down a building which is no longer needed
dog t6 simple steel fastener used in timber shoring

14

flying shore (B2d) see fig. 4

folding wedges (B2d) pair of hardwood wedges used in timber shoring

grub up (D2) remove tree roots from the ground

jack or **back shore** (B2d) see fig. 4

pick axe (B7) hand tool for loosening earth

pneumatic drill (B5) power tool for breaking up hard surfaces

needle (B2d) see fig. 4

reclaimed materials good used materials from a demolished building

raker shore (B2d) see fig. 4

rider shore (B2d) see fig. 4

scaffolding (B2d) temporary structure used in demolition; see 4.7

folding wedges

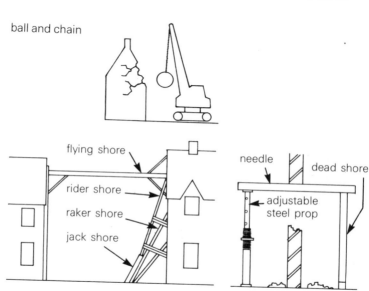

fig 4 Demolition and shoring

1.7 Setting Out (B2)

1.7.a Tools and Accessories

boning rod (B) used for laying drains to the right level; see fig. 5

builder's square (B7) see fig. 5

measuring tape (B7) see fig. 5

profile (B) used to set out trenches; see fig. 5

radius rod (B) used to set out curves; see fig. 5

sight rail (B) aid to fixing levels by eye; see fig. 5

sitesquare (A3s) simple telescope for setting out; see fig. 5

staff (A3s) see fig. 5

stake (B) see fig. 5

string or **line** (B) see fig. 5

theodolite (A3s) instrument used for setting out; see fig. 5

tripod (A3s) three-legged stand for instrument; see fig. 5

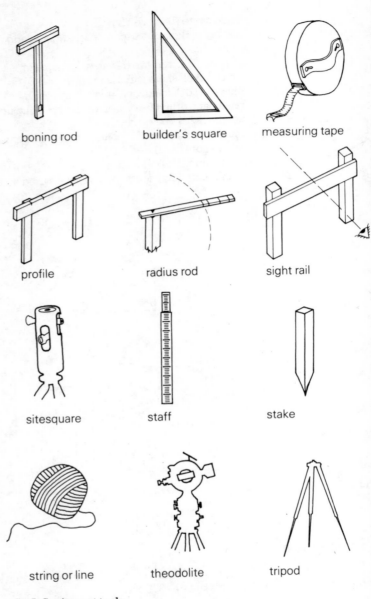

boning rod   builder's square   measuring tape

profile   radius rod   sight rail

sitesquare   staff   stake

string or line   theodolite   tripod

fig 5 Setting out tools

1.7.b Actions

levelling (A3s) measuring the height of a site at many positions

setting out (D2) marking the position of a building or part of a building on site

1.7.c General

backsight (A3s) reading taken looking back to previous theodolite position

base line (D2) line on or near site from which measurements may be taken to set out the building

diameter   radius

bench mark (A3s) known level related to sea level, usually marked on a building

contour (A3s) line joining points at the same ground level

datum (A3s) the reading at a bench mark

diameter chord passing through the centre of a circle

foresight (A3s) reading taken forwards to next theodolite position

radius half the diameter of a circle

reading (A3s) measurement taken by sighting the staff through the theodolite

site datum (A3s) datum set up on site for all site levelling

spot level (A3s) level reading at a particular point

1.8 Excavation (D)

1.8.a Tools and Plant

bulldozer (B2g) machine for scraping earth; see fig. 6

dragline (B2j) excavating machine with long reach; see fig. 6

dumper (B3e) machine for moving earth or concrete in small spaces; see fig. 6

excavator (B2j) see fig. 6

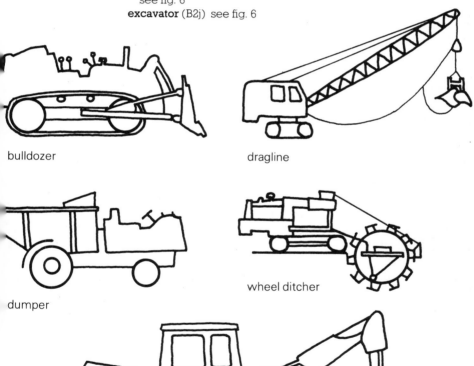

bulldozer   dragline

dumper   wheel ditcher

excavator

fig 6 **Excavation plant**

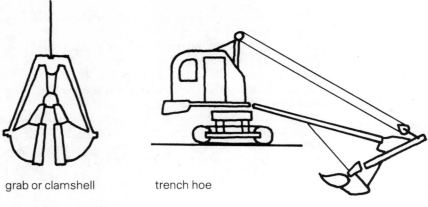

grab or clamshell   trench hoe

fig 6 Excavation plant

grab or **clamshell** (B2j) see fig. 6
tipper lorry (B3d) see fig. 6
trench hoe (B2j) machine for digging deep trenches; see fig. 6
water pump (B2t) machine with an engine which removes water by
    making it pass through a pipe
wheel ditcher (B2j) see fig. 6

1.8.b General

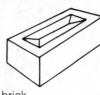

brick

gravel

sand

backfill material used to fill in a trench or excavation; see fig. 11
bearing capacity strength of earth to support a building measured in
    N/mm^2
bored piles (17) (B2r) piles driven to hold back earth and water
    during excavation
clay r firm, dense material from which bricks are made
earth pl any soft, fine material with vegetable content dug from the
    ground
formation level level of firm ground which is ready for a concrete
    slab or other construction after excavation
good bearing ground earth or other material good enough to lay a
    foundation on
gravel pl small loose stones
ground water (11.4) water in the ground
peat soft, black, fibrous earth
planking and strutting (B2d) temporary support for a trench; see fig. 7
poling board (B2d) see fig. 7
rock (11) hard ground material, eg chalk, granite, limestone,
    sandstone
sand pl tiny particles of rock
sheet piles (17) (B2r) steel piles driven to hold back earth and water
    during excavation; see fig. 7
soil pl earth
spoil pl waste earth
spoil heap pl pile of waste earth
subsoil pl see fig. 8
tip place to dispose of spoil
timbering (B2d) planking and strutting using timber boards

topsoil pl vegetable soil near the ground surface; see fig. 8
trench channel dug in the ground; see fig. 8
trial hole (A3s) hole dug to find out the materials in the ground and its
bearing capacity

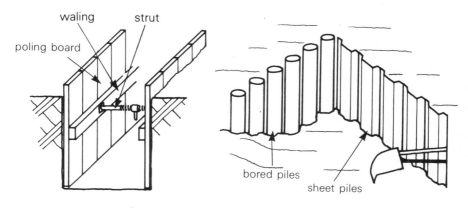

fig 7 Planking and strutting

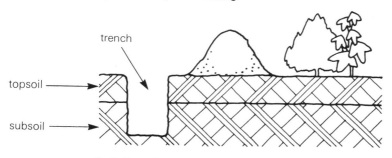

fig 8 Trench

.9 Foundations
nd Groundslabs (16)

9.a Raw Materials **aggregate** p = **gravel** pl   small stones

PFA p4   pulverised (crushed) fuel ash

sand pl   tiny rock particles

shingle pl   very small stones

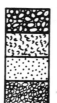

cement q2 powder from which concrete is made
hardcore p loose fill material which will not settle once compacted;
see fig. 11
ballast pl mixture of gravel, sand and grit

eg { **broken brick** g2
     broken rock p7
     large stones pl

9.b Materials   **concrete** fl material made from cement and aggregates mixed with
water, which sets hard

19

roll of polythene
sheet

readymix
concrete lorry

leanmix concrete f2 concrete without much cement in it
liquid damp-proofing material brushed on to concrete to make it
    waterproof
polythene sheet lh2 plastic sheet often laid below concrete
    groundslabs to keep out water
readymix concrete f2 concrete brought to site in a lorry
sulphate-resisting concrete f2 concrete which is not harmed by some
    chemicals in the soil which contain sulphur (chemical formula S)

1.9.c Tools and
Plant (B)

auger (B2) machine for drilling deep holes in the ground
compacting machine(B6f) device to make hardcore firm by hitting it
    again and again
concrete batching plant (B4g) machinery for mixing large batches of
    concrete; see fig. 9
monkey (B2r) heavy weight as used in some kinds of pile driver
pile driver (B2r) machine to force piles into the ground
seive (B4d) grid used for grading aggregates; see fig. 9
tower crane (B3t) see fig. 9
wheelbarrow (B3i) see fig. 9

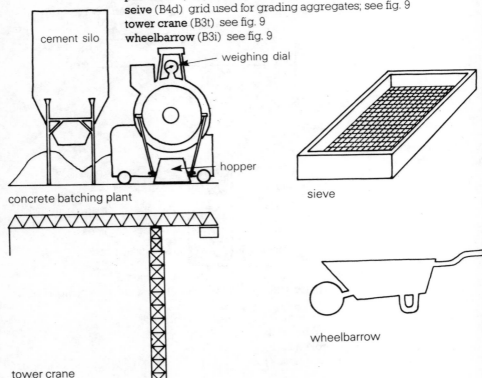

cement silo

weighing dial

hopper

concrete batching plant

sieve

tower crane

wheelbarrow

fig 9 Tools and plant for concreting

compacting concrete (D6) beating or vibrating concrete to remove pockets of air; see fig. 10

consolidating hardcore (D6) compacting hardcore; see fig. 10

floating concrete (D4) forming concrete to a smooth, level surface

measuring moisture content measuring the quantity of water in aggregates before mixing concrete

placing or **pouring concrete** (D6) see fig. 10

tamping concrete (D6) forming a surface on concrete using a long board; see fig. 10

testing concrete:

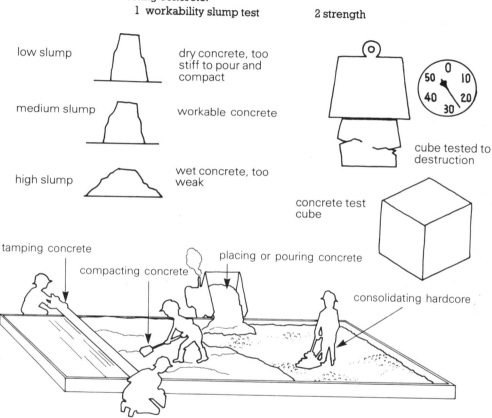

1 **workability slump test**

low slump — dry concrete, too stiff to pour and compact

medium slump — workable concrete

high slump — wet concrete, too weak

2 **strength**

cube tested to destruction

concrete test cube

tamping concrete

compacting concrete

placing or pouring concrete

consolidating hardcore

fig 10 **Laying a groundslab**

backfill material p see fig. 11

batch quantity made at one time, eg batch of concrete

blinding p layer of fine material such as sand laid on a bed of hardcore; see fig. 11

concrete groundslab (13)Ef2 see fig. 11

foundation (16) solid part of a building under the ground which transmits the load of a building to the earth

ground beam (18) see fig. 12

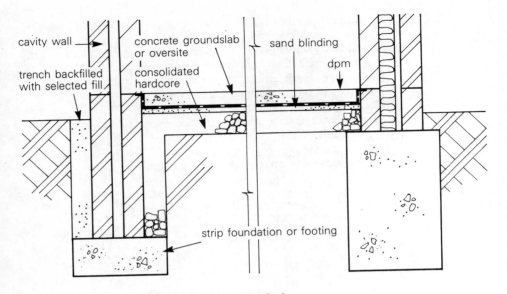

fig 11 Groundslab (section)

cavity wall

trench backfilled with selected fill

concrete groundslab or oversite

consolidated hardcore

sand blinding

dpm

strip foundation or footing

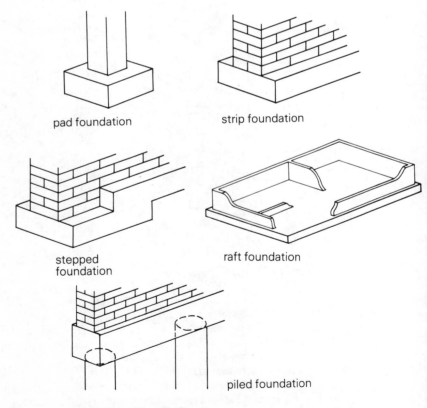

pad foundation

strip foundation

stepped foundation

raft foundation

piled foundation

fig 12 Types of foundation

made up ground ground consisting of earth or other material which
　　has been dumped on the site
oversite concrete (13.1) see fig. 11
pad foundation (16.4) see fig. 12
pile foundation (17) see fig. 12
raft foundation (16.4) see fig. 12
retaining wall (16.2) see fig. 13
settlement movement of earth due to the weight of a building
stepped foundation (16) see fig. 12
strip foundation or **footing** (16.4) see fig. 12
suspended floor floor which does not rest on the ground
tanking (16.2) waterproof structure below ground; see fig. 13
trench fill foundation (16.4) see fig. 11
underpinning (16) foundation laid below an existing building

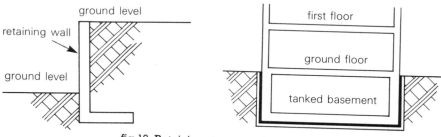

fig 13 Retaining structures (sections)

1.10 Drawings and dimensions specifications

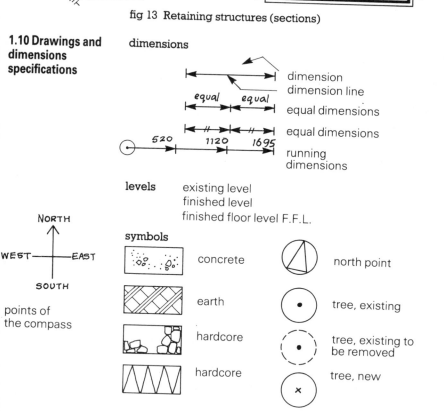

dimensions

levels　　existing level
　　　　　finished level
　　　　　finished floor level F.F.L.

points of the compass

2   Superstructure

Language Practice

2.1.a Loadbearing Walls

'Which way up does a brick go?'
One of Jack's bricklayers thinks it makes no difference which way up a brick is laid. But the architect who wrote the specification disagrees, and so does the clerk of works.

fig 14

Jack – *Foreman Bricklayer*   Sid – *Clerk of Works*   (Peter – *Site Agent*)   (Mark – *Bricklayer*)

Jack Hello, Sid. Peter said you weren't very happy about this brickwork. He asked me to sort it out with you.

Sid Yes, that's right. Young Mark started building that wall this morning, and he's laid every brick frog down as far as I can see.

Jack Oh dear. I'm sorry. Well, I'll have a word with him about it. I suppose it could have been worse, couldn't it?

Sid Well, maybe it could, but now it doesn't comply with the specification. I told him earlier on he'd have to take it down. He took no notice then – and he wasn't very polite either. I'm really annoyed about it.

Jack Well, be reasonable, Sid. I'll see he does the rest of it properly.

Sid That doesn't make any difference. It'll still have to be rebuilt, you know. There'll be voids in those frogs and there are unfilled joints everywhere. The wall just won't have adequate sound reduction.

Jack I know, I know. But surely that doesn't matter in this case, does it? It's only going to be a storeroom, after all.

Sid Well, that's not really the point. It's bad practice, and I don't want to see it happen again where it *will* matter.

Jack Well, I'm sorry, but I think you're being unreasonable.

Sid Okay, then. If that's the way you feel, I'll have to refer the matter to the architect for his decision. You can't say that's unreasonable.

adequate enough	**refer** pass on
annoyed cross	**sort (it) out** find out what's
bad practice a poor standard of work	wrong
	sound reduction the effect of a
brickwork work built with bricks	wall or floor in stopping noise from passing through it
comply with match	**specification** see 0.1
disagree have a different opinion	**storeroom** room where things are kept
frog see 2.5.e	**suppose** guess, imagine
properly correctly	**void** empty space
reasonable fair	

Answer the questions.

1 What mistake has Mark made building the wall?
2 Why is Sid annoyed?
3 Why will the wall not have adequate sound reduction?
4 Does Jack agree with Sid? What does he think about the wall?
5 What does Sid intend to do?
6 Who will have the final decision about the wall?

Fill in the blanks to complete Sid's part of the conversation.

Jack What's the matter with this wall, then, Sid?

Sid .... It'll have to be rebuilt.

Jack Well, I realise it doesn't comply with the specification, but that doesn't matter in this case, does it?

Sid .... It's not good enough.

Jack Well, I don't think that makes any difference here. We don't need sound reduction here anyway.

Sid .... And I don't want it to happen again somewhere it will matter.

Jack I'm sorry, but you're being very unreasonable if you expect us to rebuild it.

Sid .... And I hope you don't think that's being unreasonable.

2.1.b 'Have to'

'Have to' can express obligation or need.
Look at these sentences from the conversation:

I told him he'd *have to* take it down.
It'll still *have to* be rebuilt.
I'll *have to* refer the matter to the architect.

'Have to' here expresses obligation. It tells us that something needs to be done. Practise using 'have to' in this exercise. Complete the sentences with the right form of 'have to' and the verb in brackets.

Example:
Mark (build – *present*) the wall again. Jack (teach – *future*) him how to lay bricks.
Mark *has to build* the wall again. Jack *will have to teach* him how to lay bricks.

You (keep – *future*) an eye on Mark. He's laid every brick on this wall frog down. I'm afraid he (take it down – *future*). He (learn – *present*) to work to a good standard, you know. All these joints (be filled – *future*) properly, otherwise it will leave voids. I'm sorry but I (make sure – *present*) there is proper sound reduction on all these walls. And I'm afraid if you don't agree, I (go and see – *future*) the architect about it.

2.2.a Reinforced Concrete Frame

'A crisis on site'

Concrete must be handled carefully to be sure that it hardens at the right time in the right place. A breakdown in supply can cause an awkward problem.

fig 15

Tony – *Structural Engineer* Malcolm – *Concrete Engineer*
(Mick – *Groundworker*)

Malcolm Ah! hello, Tony – I hoped you wouldn't be long. We're in real trouble here.
Tony Yes, so I was told. What's the matter, then?
Malcolm Well, you see, we've poured about half of this slab, and the concrete plant's just broken down. The last load's on its way now.
Tony Oh dear. All right, let's see how far you've got. Hmm – well, it's a good job you've been pouring from one side towards the other, isn't it? It's so hard to make a neat joint if you've been pouring all over the whole area. Right, stop the pour along this line here, then. I think we'll be able to make a suitable day joint there.
Malcolm Okay. We'll get a chippie right away.

Tony Fine. Now, then, this is what I'd like you to do. Er – first of all, get a batten fixed underneath. That makes a groove, you see, which hides the joint in case it can be seen from the floor below.

Malcolm Right, I'm with you.

Tony Okay. Then shutter up the joint, in the form of a step. It helps to make a stronger joint if you do it like that.

Malcolm I think we should be able to manage that all right.

Tony Fine. And one last thing, Malcolm, don't leave any laitance on the concrete, will you? Do be sure you remove it all thoroughly. Get it off while the concrete's still fresh. Otherwise you'll get a weak finish on that concrete, see.

Malcolm Yes, I know. We'll see to that. I'll stay on late with Mick and do it.

Tony Oh, and I nearly forgot to say, you'll have to remember to apply the releasing agent properly. You know, thinly and evenly. Then you'll be able to strike the shuttering easily tomorrow, see.

Malcolm Right, okay. We'll get Mick to do a special job on it, then!

Tony Yes . . . well, we'll see how good a job you've made of it all tomorrow.

Malcolm Right, then. Well, thanks very much, Tony.

Tony Oh, that's all right.

apply put on	**fresh** new
awkward difficult	**groove** small channel
batten *see* 5.5.b	**handle** treat
breakdown failure	**laitance** *see* 2.6.d
chippie site word for carpenter; *see* 0.1	**releasing agent** *see* 2.6.a
	shuttering *see* 2.6.d
concrete *see* 1.9.b	**special** really good, extra careful
concrete plant *see* 1.9.c	
concrete batching plant	**strike** take off, take down
day joint *see* 2.6.d	**suitable** convenient
evenly smoothly	**thoroughly** completely

Answer the questions.

1 Why is it such a problem when the concrete plant breaks down?
2 How has the concrete been poured so far?
3 Why does Tony want a batten fixed underneath?
4 How will they manage to make a strong joint?
5 What will they do to strike the shuttering easily?
6 Why must they remove the laitance thoroughly? Who is going to do this?

Complete these sentences.

1 Malcolm can't pour the rest of the concrete because . . . . . .
2 It's a good thing they've been pouring the concrete from one side towards the other because . . . . . .
3 They'll be able to hide the joint from below if they . . . . . .
4 They have to shutter up the joint in the form of a step because . . . . . .
5 If they don't apply the releasing agent thinly and evenly then . . . . . .
6 The concrete will not have a good finish if . . . . . .

2.2.b Using the imperative

Look at these sentences from the conversation:

Stop the pour along this line.

Get a batten fixed underneath.

Don't leave any laitance on the concrete.

The imperative form is used for instructions, commands, warnings – sometimes persuasion. We form the negative imperative with 'don't' (or 'do not'). To be more polite or persuasive we can add 'please' at the beginning or end of the sentence. Practise using imperatives in this exercise.

Example:

Tell Malcolm to get a carpenter straight away.

Get a carpenter straight away, Malcolm.

1 Ask Tony to come and give you some advice.
2 Persuade Mick to stay and remove the laitance.
3 Get Peter to come and see what's wrong.
4 Tell the carpenter to shutter up this joint as soon as he can.
5 Remind Malcolm to remove the shuttering in the morning.
6 Ask Tony to have a look at the groove underneath next time he's on site.

2.3.a Steel Frame

'Seeing a mistake is the first step in rectifying it'

When a component has been made incorrectly, it is best to find a solution which doesn't create more problems.

fig 16

Ted }
Bob } *Steel Erectors*   (Harry – *Foreman Steel Erector*)

Bob Look, Ted, the bolt holes in this stanchion don't tie up with the drawing. They're on the wrong side or something ,aren't they?

Ted So they are. Hey, you know, all the other stanchions on this side are wrong as well, by the look of it. Oh, no!

Bob Someone must have made a mistake, then. Everywhere else it's the side farthest from the outside wall that the beams have been bolted to, isn't it? But look, here the holes are *nearer* the outside on the stanchion.

Ted Well, there's only one way that could have happened. These stanchions must have been fixed the wrong way round.

Bob Oh dear, I expect we shall have to drill new holes then. We don't want the bearing of the concrete slabs on these beams reduced from 150 millimetres to 50 millimetres, I don't suppose.

Ted But just a minute – couldn't the slabs be moved over 25 millimetres instead? Then the gap at the other end could be filled with concrete, couldn't it?

Bob Oh, I wouldn't advise that. The external cladding is separate from these floor beams, but there might be services running in the space in between, you see. There wouldn't be enough room for that if you moved the slabs over at all.

Ted Hmm – I suppose you're right. Well, perhaps we'd better have a word with Harry.

Bob Okay – I'll go then. And you go and check over the drill. I think we'll probably be needing it.

beam *see* 2.7.a **floor beam**
bearing area which a beam rests on at its ends
bolt hole hole through which a bolt is fixed
component part
drill machine for making holes *see* 5.5.c
external cladding panels fixed to the outside of a building

gap space
rectify put right
reduce make less, make smaller
separate from not joined to
service gas, water, electricity, etc, in a building
slab *see* 2.6.d **flat slab floor**
stanchion *see* 2.7.a
tie up with match

Answer the questions.
1 What problem have the steel erectors found?
2 Why don't the bolt holes on the stanchion tie up with the drawing?
3 Why does Bob think they will have to drill new holes?
4 What does Ted suggest they could do?
5 Where does Bob think there may be services running?
6 What do they decide to do about it?

Fill in the blanks.
Ted and Bob are working on . . . . . . They find that . . . . . . They can't bolt the beams to these stanchions because . . . . . . Ted suggests . . . . . but Bob thinks it might not work because . . . . . . They think they will probably have to . . . . . , so Ted goes to . . . . . while Bob goes to see Harry, the foreman.

2.3.b 'Must have'

'Must have' is used to express certainty about the past. Look at these sentences from the conversation:

Someone *must have made* a mistake.

These stanchions *must have been fixed* the wrong way round.

In these sentences 'must have' expresses firm belief about something that happened in the past. The speaker was not actually there to see what happened, but he is certain about what happened because of things he now knows. Practise 'must have' in this exercise, using the words in brackets ( ) to make your sentence. Start each sentence with 'Someone'.

Example:
These bolt holes don't tie up with the drawing. (drill; the holes; in the wrong place)
Someone must have drilled the holes in the wrong place.

1 The bolt holes in the stanchion are nearer the outside of the building. (fix; the stanchions; the wrong way round)

2 The bearing on these beams is only 50 mm. (fix; the beams; in the wrong place)

3 There isn't enough space for the service pipes in here. (make; a mistake; with the floor beams)

4 This gap has been filled with concrete. (move; the slabs; further over)

5 Harry's coming out to look at the holes in the stanchions. (tell; him; about the problem)

6 The men are bringing the drill over. (ask; them; to drill new holes)

Communication on Site

Giving instructions and warnings

2.4.a Instructions

Giving instructions is extremely important on site. Sometimes people have to be taught how to do jobs correctly. Sometimes instructions have to be given quickly to prevent a disaster or accident.

In conversation 2.2.a, Tony is giving some instructions to Malcolm in a crisis situation. Look at how he does this. Sometimes he uses the imperative form (see 2.2.b). He also uses longer forms of instruction:

Do be sure you remove it all thoroughly.

You'll have to remember to apply the releasing agent properly.
Other ways he could give instructions are:

Take care to	Be careful not to . . . . .
You'll have to	You won't have to . . . . .
I'd like you to	I don't want you to . . . . .
You'd better	You'd better not . . . . .
Make sure you remember to	Don't forget to . . . . .

Practise using the imperative and longer forms of instruction by telling Mick what to do in this exercise. Each time begin by using an imperative, and then try using a different way of giving the same instructions.

Example:
Tell him to get the concrete covered to keep the rain out.
A *Get that concrete covered to keep the rain out, Mick!*
B *Make sure you get the concrete covered to keep the rain out, Mick.*

1 Tell him to start pouring concrete.
2 Tell him not to pour it over the whole area.
3 Tell him to bring the drill to make some new holes.
4 Tell him not to strike the shuttering yet.
5 Tell him to stay on late to remove all the laitance.
6 Tell him to help Mark to take down the brick wall.

2.4.b. Point-by-point instructions

When we give a series of instructions, we usually list them, as Tony does in conversation 2.2.a. This makes what we are saying clearer and easier to remember. Here are some ways to give point-by-point instructions:

First of all	First . . . . .
Then	And then . . . . .
The next thing is	Next . . . . .
After you've done that	One last thing . . . . .
And finally	Last of all . . . . .

Sometimes we forget one of the instructions, and have to add it at the end. How does Tony do this in the conversation? Practise giving point-by-point instructions in this exercise.
Here are some instructions about bricklaying taken from a book:
1 Choose a good, unchipped brick.
2 Pick up brick in left hand.
3 Spread mortar on surface where brick is to be laid.
4 Butter mortar on brick-end.
5 Place brick flat side down, frog upwards, against last-laid brick.
6 Smooth off joint with trowel.
Use these instructions to make a clear, point-by-point explanation, such as Jack might give to Mark on site to teach him the correct way to lay bricks. Begin like this:
First of all, choose a good, unchipped brick and pick it up in your left hand. Then . . .

2.4.c. Other forms of instruction

Written instructions are usually given as imperatives:

Fix bracket to stanchion at A.
Drill holes at points A and B.
In an urgent crisis situation we often give our instructions in imperatives too. (Look again at conversation 2.2.a.) But when we are just giving general instructions on site, or showing someone how to do something, we often prefer to avoid the imperative altogether, and instead we use constructions like:

You have to You've got to	fix the bracket to the stanchion at A.
You should drill You drill	holes at points A and B.

Practise these forms like this: imagine again that you are Jack, and give Mark instructions for laying bricks the correct way, this time avoiding the imperative in your explanations.

2.4.d Warnings

Warnings are given as short, sharp imperatives in situations where there is likelihood of danger or accident, or where immediate attention is needed:

Keep away from the edge!
Be careful!
Don't step on that concrete!
Watch out!
Mind! Mind you don't fall!
Stand back!

But warnings can also be used to guard against the possibility of danger rather than to warn of the actual danger itself:

Do be careful to keep away from that concrete.
Make sure you don't go near the edge.
Mind you fix your ladder properly before you go up.
Don't forget to keep your tools well away from the edge.

The tone of your voice as well as your words will be important in showing which kind of warning you are giving.

Describe what is going on in each of the pictures below. Then give the words of warning spoken in each situation.

Example:
Mark is going up a ladder that has not been tied to the scaffolding. Peter tells him to make it safe.

example

2.5 Loadbearing Walls (2–)

2.5.a Materials

cement q2 powder which hardens when mixed with water
clay g2 most common material for making bricks
lime q1 white powder used in mortar (chemical formula CaO)
lime putty q1 hydrated lime, ie lime mixed with water (chemical formula Ca(OH))
mastic t4 substance used for pointing joints in brickwork, eg expansion joints
mortar q4 binding material for use with bricks and blocks
plasticiser u2 liquid admixture to improve the workability of mortar
stone e natural building material quarried from the ground, eg granite, marble, sandstone

2.5.b Components

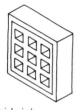
airbrick

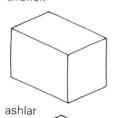
ashlar

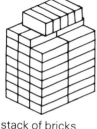
stack of bricks

airbrick Fg2 brick allowing air to pass through it
ashlar or **ashler** Fe piece of stone cut square
bat Fg2 a cut brick, eg half bat; three-quarter bat
concrete block Ff building block made of concrete
concrete boot lintol (3–) Hf see fig. 17
brick Fg2 hand-sized building block, mostly made from clay
butterfly tie h wall tie; see fig. 18
calcium silicate brick Ff1 sandlime or flintlime brick made from sand and lime
cellular brick Fg2 see fig. 19
common brick Fg2 low cost brick not used as a facing brick
concrete brick Ff brick made from concrete
damp proof course Ff layer of material through which moisture cannot pass
dressed stone Fe stone cut square, with smooth face
engineering brick Fg2 strong, dense clay brick, which does not allow much water to get inside it
facing brick F brick with good appearance
fair-faced concrete block Ff block with good appearance

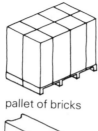
pallet of bricks

roll of damp proof course (dpc)

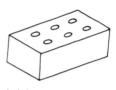
brick

concrete block

foundation stone

fixing brick Fi1 wooden brick built into a wall as a joinery fixing

cramp t6 metal fixing screwed to a window or door frame and built into brickwork

flintlime brick Ff1 calcium silicate brick

foundation stone Fe stone with carved lettering built into a wall

half bat F half brick

handmade brick Fg2 brick shaped by hand instead of by a machine

hollow brick Fg2 see fig. 19

lightweight steel lintol (3–)Hh2 see fig. 17

lintol or lintel (3–)H structural support over an opening in a loadbearing wall

lintol block Ff precast block from which a reinforced concrete lintol may be made; see fig. 17

machine pressed brick F brick shaped by machine

metric modular brick Fg2 metric size brick, eg 290 × 90 × 90 mm

perforated brick Fg2 see fig. 19

sandlime brick Ff1 calcium silicate brick

screen wall block Ff see fig. 20

solid brick Fg2 see fig. 19

snap header Fg2 half bat used as a header in a half brick wall

special brick F brick of unusual shape made to special order

standard special brick F much used special brick which most manufacturers keep in stock; see fig. 21

steel strap t6 fixing built into brickwork and fixed to roof or floor members

twin triangle tie h brick tie; see fig. 18

twisted steel tie h brick tie; see fig. 18

wirecut brick Fg2 brick made by a machine which cuts the face of the brick with wire; see fig. 19

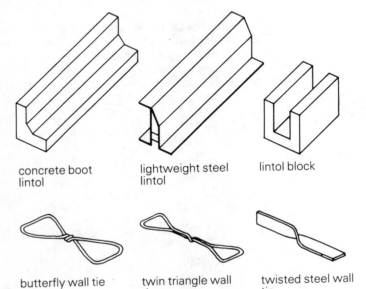

fig 17 Lintols

concrete boot lintol

lightweight steel lintol

lintol block

butterfly wall tie

twin triangle wall tie

twisted steel wall tie

fig 18 Wall ties

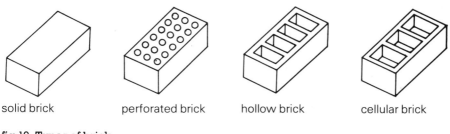

solid brick   perforated brick   hollow brick   cellular brick

fig 19 Types of brick

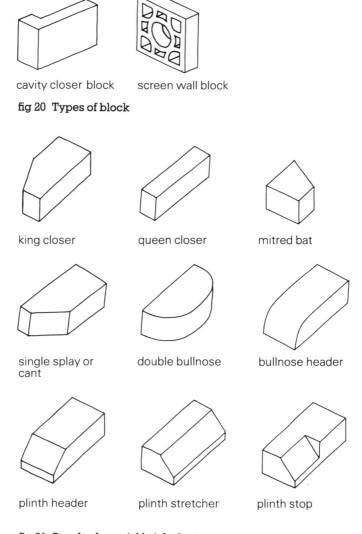

cavity closer block   screen wall block

fig 20 Types of block

king closer   queen closer   mitred bat

single splay or cant   double bullnose   bullnose header

plinth header   plinth stretcher   plinth stop

fig 21 Standard special brick shapes

2.5.c Tools and Plant

bevel (B7) see fig. 22
bolster (B7) tool for cutting bricks; see fig. 22
bricklayer's hammer(B7) see fig. 22
brick trowel (B7) see fig. 22
brickwork chaser (B7) power machine for cutting grooves in brickwork in which to fix pipes for other services; see fig. 23
carborundum saw (B7) brickwork chaser; see fig. 23
cement mixer (B4a) see fig. 23
hawk (B7) board on which mortar is carried; see fig. 22
hod (B7) device to carry bricks manually; see fig. 22
hoist (B3w) machine to carry bricks from one level to another; see fig. 23
jointer (B7) tool for finishing brick joints; see fig. 22
keyway miller (B7) brick chaser; see fig. 23
line pins (B7) see fig. 22
mastic gun (B7) tool for putting mastic into a joint; the mastic is forced out through a nozzle
mortar scoop (B7) tool for forming thin joints; see fig. 22
plumb rule (B7) tool to check that brickwork is vertical; see fig. 22
scaffolding (B2d) see 4.7
spirit level (B7) tool to check that brickwork is horizontal; see fig. 22
try square (B7) tool to check that a corner is square; see fig. 22

nozzle

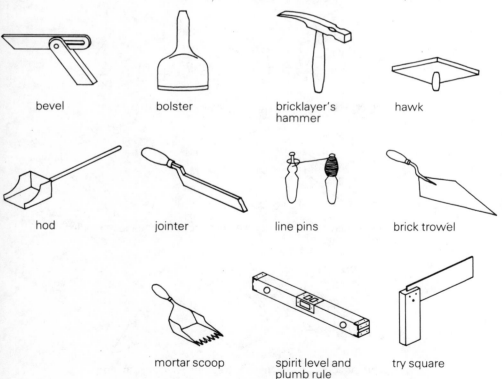

bevel   bolster   bricklayer's hammer   hawk

hod   jointer   line pins   brick trowel

mortar scoop   spirit level and plumb rule   try square

fig 22 Bricklaying tools

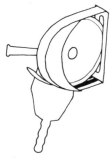

brickwork chaser

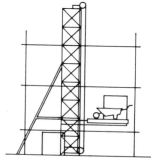

hoist

cement mixer

fig 23 Plant for bricklaying and brickwork

2.5.d Actions

beam filling F(D6) building a wall up between the ends of joists or beams

bonding brickwork F (D6) laying bricks so as to break the joints, to form a strong wall

breaking joint F(D6) laying a brick so as to cover the joint below, which avoids a straight joint

building in F(D6) building brickwork around a door or window frame, or other item; eg windows to be built into external wall

buttering a brick F(D6) applying mortar to a brick before laying it; see fig. 24

fair cutting F(D4) cutting a brick cleanly where the cut edge will be seen

fair cut brick

laying bricks F(D6) the process of building bricks into a wall using mortar

overhand bricklaying F(D6) laying facing bricks to an external wall from inside the building; see fig. 25

pointing brickwork F(D6) filling joints in brickwork with mortar; often needed on old brickwork

rough cutting F(D4) cutting a brick quickly, when the cut edge will not be seen

rough cut brick

setting out bond preparing to lay bricks by measuring the lengths of wall needed

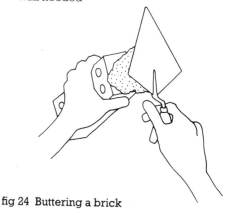

fig 24 Buttering a brick

fig 25 Laying bricks overhand

faced brickwork

2.5.e General

arch (2–) see fig. 26

ashlar or ashler e wall built of stone cut square and laid in courses

brick bond F a pattern for laying bricks to build a strong, bonded wall of regular appearance, eg Flemish bond, Stretcher bond

cavity-fill insulation by means of pumping material into a brick cavity

cavity wall (21.1) two walls with a space (cavity) between them; see fig. 26

compartment wall (22.8) wall able to stop fire passing through it

control joint Z see **expansion joint**

corbel F see fig. 26

course horizontal layer of bricks, blocks or stone; see fig. 26

diagonal bond F see fig. 27

efflorescence white stain on brickwork caused by salts, especially when drying out

English bond F see fig. 27

expansion joint Z straight joint in a wall which allows movement caused by heat or moisture

fat mix q2 mortar containing more cement than usual

Flemish bond F see fig. 27

flush joint Z see fig. 28

frog recess in a brick

gauge F vertical measurement of brickwork, eg four courses = 300 mm

half brick wall F see fig. 26

header face F the end face of a brick

herringbone bond F see **diagonal bond**

indent F hole left in a wall so that another wall may be bonded into it later; see fig. 26

joint Z bed of mortar joining two bricks

lean mix q2 mortar containing less cement than usual

lift brickwork built before scaffolding needs to be erected or raised, eg 'first lift'; 'second lift'

mortar bed q2 layer of mortar on which a brick or other item is laid

mortar droppings q2 lumps of mortar which drop into a cavity; these must be removed from the wall ties

natural bed e the direction in which a piece of stone was lying in its natural position before being quarried; stone is often laid in a building to its natural bed

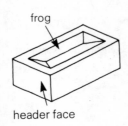

frog

header face

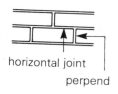
horizontal joint

perpend

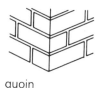
quoin

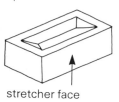
stretcher face

neat cement q2 mortar made from cement and water only

one brick wall F see fig. 26

pallet (B3) wooden base; bricks are stacked on to it for transport

parapet (21.8) wall built around a roof; see fig. 26

party wall (22.8) wall between two houses or other buildings, and jointly owned

perpend Z perpendicular joint

quoin F the corner of a wall

raking bond F see **diagonal bond**

recessed joint Z see fig. 28

reinforced brickwork or **blockwork** F wall of hollow bricks or blocks with steel rods and concrete built into it

reveal brick F see fig. 27

rough work F brickwork which can be built quickly because it will not be seen

rounded joint Z see fig. 28

rubble wall e stone wall; the stones are not cut square and laid in even courses

separating wall (22.8) party wall

stretcher bond F see fig. 27

stretcher face F the side face of a brick

struck joint Z see fig. 28

weather struck joint Z see fig. 28

weephole space or pipe built into a retaining wall to allow water to pass through

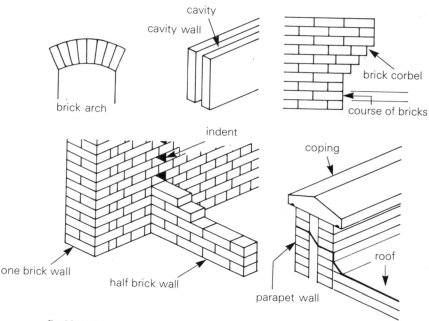

fig 26 Brickwork

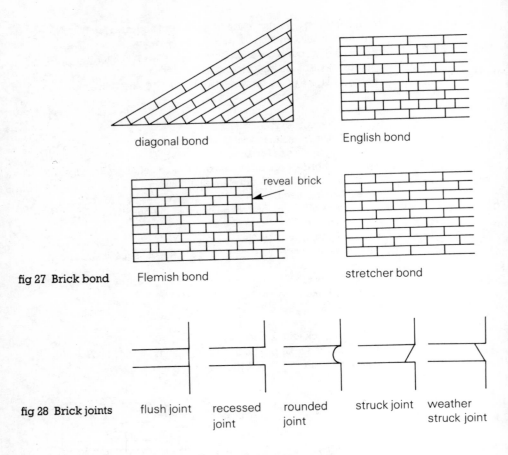

diagonal bond

English bond

reveal brick

fig 27 Brick bond   Flemish bond

stretcher bond

fig 28 Brick joints   flush joint   recessed joint   rounded joint   struck joint   weather struck joint

2.6 Reinforced Concrete Frames (28)

2.6.a Materials and Components

See also Unit One Reference Section (1.9.a and 1.9.b)

admixture u2 liquid or powder which gives concrete a certain property, eg makes it waterproof
aerated concrete f concrete cast with air bubbles in it
binding wire Jh wire used to fix reinforcement bars together
cable Jh thick steel thread made from many wires; used in post-tensioned concrete
cable duct Ih steel tube to contain post-tensioning cable
concrete floor slab Gf see fig. 29
end block fixing block for cable in post-tensioned concrete
hessian Tj3 coarse fabric used to cover concrete whilst curing

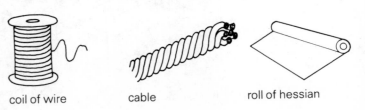

coil of wire   cable   roll of hessian

lightweight concrete f5 concrete with light aggregates or with air
bubbles in it

mould oil z oil brushed on to formwork; it makes the formwork easier
to remove afterwards

pan piece of formwork used to cast a waffle slab; see fig. 30

pot F concrete or clay block used in a beam and pot floor; see fig. 34

reinforcement cage h see fig. 31

releasing agent see 'mould oil'

ring spacer f kind of spacer block

spacer block f very small concrete block used to keep
reinforcement bars off the bottom of the formwork

steel reinforcement bar Hh:

stirrup or **binder** see fig. 31

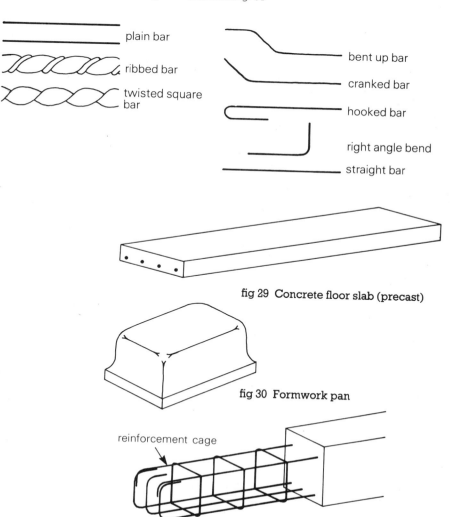

ring spacer

plain bar

ribbed bar

twisted square
bar

bent up bar

cranked bar

hooked bar

right angle bend

straight bar

fig 29 Concrete floor slab (precast)

fig 30 Formwork pan

reinforcement cage

fig 31 Reinforcement cage

2.6.b Tools and Plant

See also Unit One Reference Section (1.9.c)

bending machine (B5g) machine for bending reinforcement bars

chute (B) see fig. 32

concrete pump (B) machine to force concrete through a long pipe

external vibrator (B6g) device fixed to the outside of formwork to vibrate the concrete

hammer (B7) pneumatic or electric tool for removing concrete or making holes in it; see fig. 32

jack tool (B) for tightening cables in post-tensioned concrete

pliers (pair of) (B7) hand tool which can cut wire; see fig. 32

poker vibrator (B6g) hand-held tool to remove air pockets and air bubbles from concrete after pouring; see fig. 32

prop pole to support bottom of formwork while concrete hardens

wire cutter(B7) hand tool for cutting wire

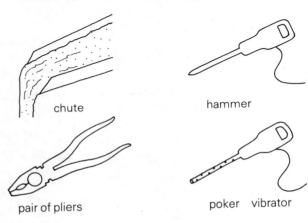

chute
hammer
pair of pliers
poker vibrator

fig 32 Tools for reinforced concrete

2.6.c Actions

See also Unit One Reference Section (1.9.d)

casting concrete q(D6) the process of filling a mould or formwork with concrete

concreting q(D6) the process of mixing and pouring concrete

curing concrete keeping concrete moist while it hardens

erecting formwork R(D6) fixing formwork in place ready for concreting

shuttering up R(D6) erecting formwork

steam curing curing concrete with steam to reduce surface cracking

steel bending Hh(D4) shaping reinforcement bars

steelfixing Hh(D6) putting reinforcement bars in place for concreting

striking formwork removing formwork when concrete has hardened

vibrating concrete see fig. 33

2.6.d General

see also Unit One Reference Section (1.9.e)

arris corner edge; see fig. 36

batten il length of timber used to cast a groove at a construction joint

batten

beam and slab floor (23.2)Eq see fig. 34

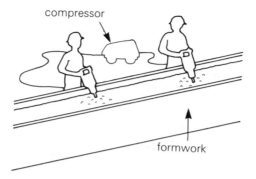

fig 33 **Vibrating concrete**

bay area of concrete flooring poured at one time
cantilever structure with no support at one end or on one side; see
    fig. 35
cast-in-situ concrete Eq concrete cast in the place it is needed
coffered slab (23.2)Eq see fig. 34
column head (28)q see fig. 36
concrete membrane (27.6)Eq thin layer of concrete in a concrete
    shell

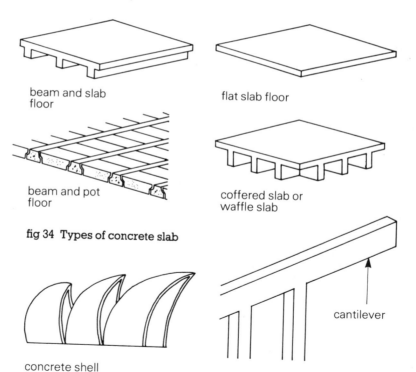

beam and slab
floor

flat slab floor

beam and pot
floor

coffered slab or
waffle slab

fig 34 **Types of concrete slab**

concrete shell
(Sydney Opera House)

cantilever

fig 35 **Concrete forms**

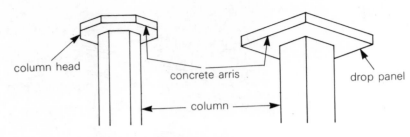

fig 36 Concrete columns

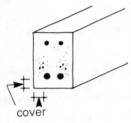

cover

concrete shell (27.6)Eq building formed by a thin curved layer of
   reinforced concrete; see fig. 35
construction joint Z joint made between parts of a concrete wall or
   floor cast at different times
cover thickness of concrete covering steel reinforcement; eg 40 mm
   cover
day joint Z construction joint made at the end of a day pouring
   concrete
drop panel (28)q see fig. 36
flat slab floor (23.2)Eq see fig. 34
green concrete q new concrete which has not cured
groove long narrow recess
grout cement and water; grout runs out of formwork which has not
   been sealed
helical reinforcement h see fig. 37
laitance layer of watery cement which forms on the top surface of
   concrete as it hardens; laitance is removed when making a
   construction joint
lap overlap where two reinforcement bars are joined; eg 300 mm lap
lift height of a wall or column cast at one time, eg half of one storey
permanent shuttering formwork which is not removed after casting
   concrete
precast concrete Eq concrete cast in a factory and transported to the
   place it is needed
pre-stressed concrete (28)q concrete beam or slab in which the
   reinforcement bars are stretched before casting

lap

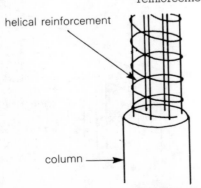

fig 37 Helical reinforcement

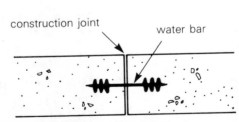

fig 38 Construction joint (plan)

segregated
concrete

pre-tensioned concrete (28)q pre-stressed concrete
post-tensioned concrete (28)q concrete structure in which the
    reinforcement is stretched after the concrete has hardened
scale loose steel often found on reinforcement bars when delivered
    to site
segregation separation of aggregates from grout in concrete
soffit underside of concrete floor or beam
timber grounds it wood cast into concrete as a fixing for joinery
waffle slab(23.2)Eq see fig. 34
water bar see fig. 38

2.7.a Steel Frames
(28)Hh

Materials and
Components

anchor bolt ht6 bolt with one end to be cast into concrete
black bolt ht6 bolt which does not fit tightly the hole it passes through
bolt ht6 fixing used with a nut
bulb flat Hh2 steel section
castellated beam (28)h see fig. 39
flat steel Hh2 length of plate steel
floor beam (28)Hh see fig. 39
friction grip bolt ht6 bolt made from high strength steel
girder (28)Hh large beam
lattice beam (28)Hh see fig. 39
lock nut ht6 nut screwed tight against another nut
nut ht6 hexagonal ring which screws onto a bolt
plate girder (28)Hh large steel girder
primary roof beam (27)h see fig. 39
rectangular hollow section Hh2 steel tube
red lead paint Vv1 red primer paint applied to steelwork after
    fabrication
rolled steel joist Hh2 (RSJ) steel beam
round section Hh2 steel tube
seating cleat or **stool** (28)h2 see fig. 40
secondary roof beam (27)h2 see fig. 39
splice plate (28)Hh2 steel plate used to join two other plates together;
    see fig. 40
square hollow section Hh2 steel tube
stanchion (28)Hh2 steel column; see fig. 39
stanchion base plate (28)h2 plate to fix a stanchion to a concrete
    foundation

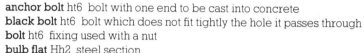

weld

plate girder

bolt

bulb flat

flat steel

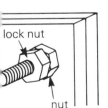

lock nut

nut

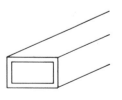

rectangular
hollow section

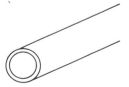

round section

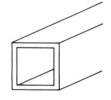

square hollow
section

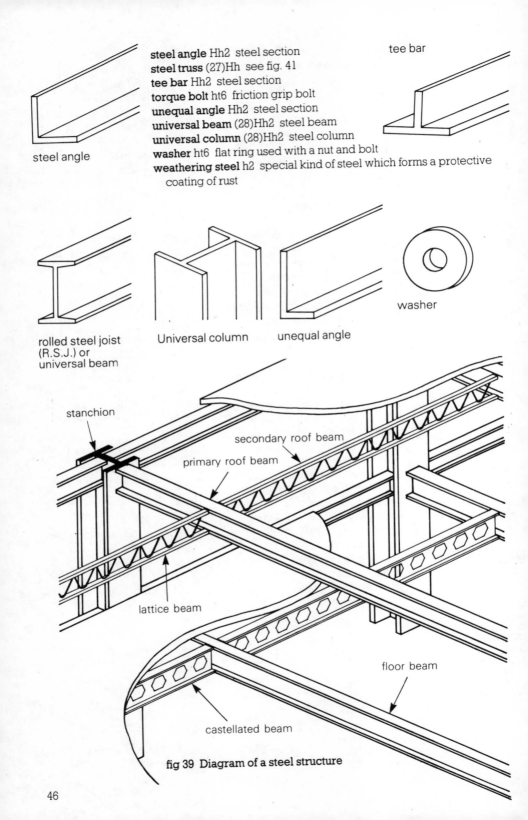

steel angle Hh2 steel section
steel truss (27)Hh see fig. 41
tee bar Hh2 steel section
torque bolt ht6 friction grip bolt
unequal angle Hh2 steel section
universal beam (28)Hh2 steel beam
universal column (28)Hh2 steel column
washer ht6 flat ring used with a nut and bolt
weathering steel h2 special kind of steel which forms a protective
    coating of rust

tee bar

steel angle

rolled steel joist
(R.S.J.) or
universal beam

Universal column

unequal angle

washer

stanchion

secondary roof beam

primary roof beam

lattice beam

floor beam

castellated beam

fig 39 Diagram of a steel structure

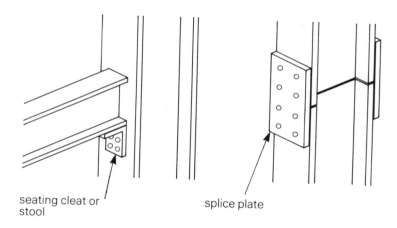

seating cleat or
stool

splice plate

fig 40 Joints in steelwork

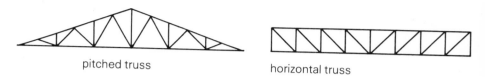

pitched truss

horizontal truss

fig 41 Types of steel truss

2.7.b *Tools and
Plant*

adjustable spanner (B7) see fig. 42
crane (B3v) see fig. 42
ring spanner (B7) see fig. 42
spanner (B7) see fig. 42
torque wrench (B7) kind of spanner which tightens a bolt to the right
tightness
tower crane (B3v) see fig. 9

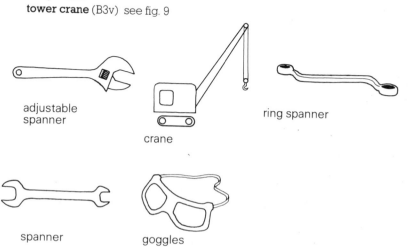

adjustable
spanner

crane

ring spanner

spanner

goggles

fig 42 Tools and plant for steelwork

2.7.c Actions

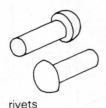

rivets

2.7.e General

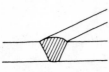

butt weld

deflection

aligning stanchions (D6) casting anchor bolts for steel stanchions into concrete foundations in the right place

bolting (D6) fixing and tightening nuts and bolts

erecting steelwork (D6) · bolting or welding a steel frame together on site

fabricating steelwork making the parts of a steel frame at a factory

riveting (D4) fixing rivets using a riveting machine

shot blasting cleaning steel by blowing hard particles on to it very fast

welding (D4) using molten (melted) steel to join two pieces of steel together

butt weld Zh2 type of welded joint

column splice Zh2 joint in a steel column; see fig. 40

connection Zh2 joint between any two parts of a steel frame

deflection movement of a beam when loaded

encased covered up; steel columns and beams are often encased to protect them from fire

fillet weld Zh2 type of welded joint

flange part of a steel beam or column

mill finish as made at the steelworks, ie without primer paint or other finish

mill scale particles of steel on the surface of new steelwork

portal frame (28.2) type of building structure; see fig. 43

rust red/brown coating formed on steel when it gets wet

space frame or **grid** (27.6)Hh see fig. 43

space frame joint (27.6)Hh see fig. 43

thread part of a bolt which makes a nut wind on to it

web part of a steel beam or column

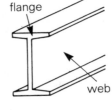

flange

web

lap weld

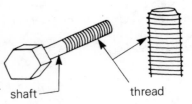

shaft

thread

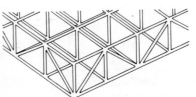

portal frame

space frame

space frame joint

fig 43 Steel roof structures

2.8 Timber framed Buildings (28)i

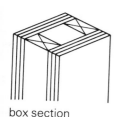

box section
column

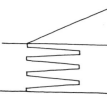

finger joint

adhesive t3 glue; laminated beam is made of strips of wood glued together

box section column (28)Hi type of timber column

finger joint Zi type of glued timber joint

framing Hi lengths of timber forming a frame

framing anchor Zh2 bent steel plate used at joints in timber framing

lamella structure (27.6)i curved structure formed from short lengths of timber fixed together by bolts or timber connectors

laminated timber beam (28)i beam made from strips of timber fixed together with adhesive

metal plate gusset Zh metal timber connector

plywood box beam (28)i beam made from timber and plywood; see fig. 44

plywood box portal frame (28.2)i see fig. 44

sheathing Ri part of a structural wall panel; see fig. 45

spaced column (28)Hi type of timber column

stressed skin panel (23)Gi see fig. 45

structural wall panel (21)G prefabricated loadbearing timber wall; see fig. 45

stud wall (22)Hi timber wall constructed in-situ (in position)

timber wood: material cut from trees

timber connector Zh2 steel fixing for jointing timber

timber roof truss (27.9)i see fig. 46

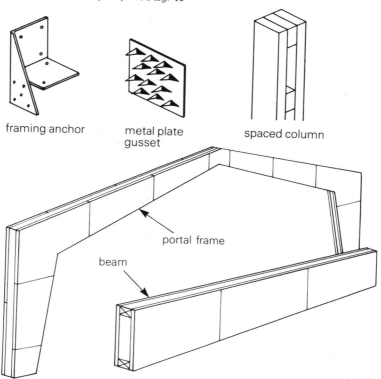

framing anchor   metal plate gusset   spaced column

portal frame

beam

fig 44 Plywood box structures

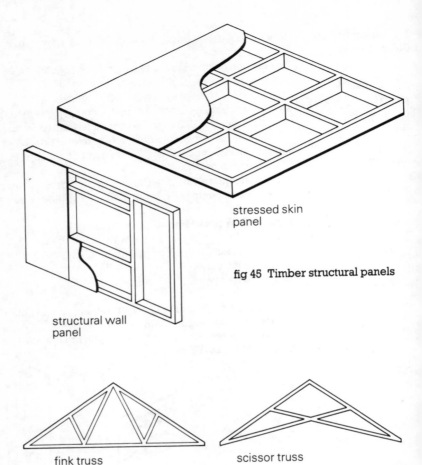

stressed skin
panel

fig 45 Timber structural panels

structural wall
panel

fink truss

scissor truss

fig 46 Types of timber roof truss

2.9 Drawing Conventions

2.9.a Drawings (A3t)

Layout plan of a steel frame

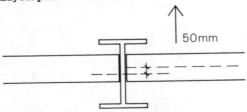

50mm

the arrow indicates the *eccentricity* of the beam fixed to the column

Reinforcement schedule list describing all reinforcement bars
required for a reinforced concrete structure

Shop drawing drawing made by a steelwork supplier for fabrication
of the steelwork in his factory workshop

*2.9.b Symbols
(A3t)*

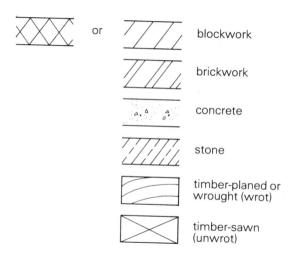

or   blockwork

brickwork

concrete

stone

timber-planed or
wrought (wrot)

timber-sawn
(unwrot)

plywood

3 Roof

Language Practice

3.1.a Pitched Roof (Traditional)

'We learn by our mistakes'
It is a good site agent who can ensure that all work is properly supervised at all times. Small faults may go unnoticed until it is too late to avoid a lot of extra work.

fig 47

Peter – *Site Agent*   Jack – *Foreman Bricklayer*

Peter Hey, Jack, the tiler has just pointed out this roof to me. Do you see anything wrong with it?

Jack Oh yes, now you come to mention it. It looks as if the ridge is kind of sagging, doesn't it?

Peter That's right. The tiler thought perhaps the roof trusses weren't strong enough, or something. But as I told him, roof trusses always drop a little after tiling.

Jack Hmm – so it's those party walls, then, I suppose they've been taken up a bit too far. The trusses either side won't have been able to drop.

Peter Exactly. And something's got to be done about it, you know. I must say, I think you ought to give those young bricklayers a few lessons. We can't have this sort of thing happening every time you take a week's holiday, can we?

Jack Okay, Peter, I'll put them right. Er – I'll get them to take twenty-five millimetres or so off those two party walls, and check over all the rest up there.

Peter Yes – that'll be all right. And I'll get the tiler to strip back the roof tiles where you'll need to get underneath. Now, I want that roof looking decent by the end of the day.

Jack Right, we'll see what we can do then.

adjacent next to
avoid not have to do
decent up to the right standard
drop sink down
ensure make sure
mention say
party wall see 2.5.e
pitched see 3.6.d **pitch**

ridge see 3.6.d
roof truss see 3.6.d **truss**
sag sink in the middle
strip back take off
supervise keep a check on
tiler person who lays tiles; see 0.1
traditional in the usual style
unnoticed without being seen

Answer the questions.

1 What has the tiler pointed out to Peter?
2 What always happens to roof trusses after tiling?
3 How have some of the trusses been prevented from dropping?
4 When did the bricklayers make their mistake?
5 What will Jack have to get the men to do?
6 When does Peter expect the problem to be sorted out?

Fill in the blanks in the conversation.

Jack What's wrong with this roof, then, Peter?
Peter Well, ...
Jack Well, aren't the roof trusses strong enough or something?
Peter ....
Jack Oh, I see. So it's the party walls, then. The men have built them up too high.
Peter Yes, ...
Jack Yes, of course. I'll get them to sort it out straight away. How much should we take off?
Peter Well, ...
Jack Okay, then, and while they're up there they can check over all the other party walls at the same time.
Peter Right, ...
Jack Fine, I'll wait till he finishes stripping them back before I send the men up again.

3.1.b How to use 'get'

Look at these sentences:

> Would you *get the tiler to strip* back the tiles?
> *Get the bricklayers to come* down in this wind!
> I'd like to *get you to agree* to the alterations.
> We must *get the men to work* more carefully.

'Get' is a very common word in spoken English. Used in this way, with object person(s) and infinitive, it can have the meaning of 'tell', 'ask', 'persuade', 'command', so it is an important way of passing on messages or instructions to other people. Find the places where 'get' is used in this way in the conversation, and practise it yourself in this exercise.

Imagine you are Peter, the site agent. The sentences given below show things that need to be done. Write down the words you say to get someone to do the things, using the word in brackets ( ) as your object person. Start each time with 'Will you get . . .'.

Example:

The sagging roof must be pointed out to Jack. (the tiler)
Will you get the tiler to point out the sagging roof to Jack?

1 Something must be done about the roof. (Jack)
2 This sagging roof must be seen to. (Jack)
3 The party walls must be taken down about 25 mm. (the men)
4 The other party walls must be checked over too. (the bricklayers)
5 The roof tiles must be stripped back first. (the tiler)
6 Those bricklayers must be given a few lessons. (Jack)

3.2.a Flat Roof

'A building is as good as the men who build it'

A good builder cares about the quality of the building, and makes use of his practical experience by saying when he thinks the specification isn't good enough.

fig 48

Peter – *Site Agent* Norman – *Architect*

Peter Well, now, my last point is about the falls you've indicated on the flat roof of the office building.

Norman Oh yes, let's see. It's drawing number L(27)5. Er – here it is.

Peter Now, you've shown the high and low points and personally I'd like to see greater falls on here. Er – I hope you don't mind my mentioning it.

Norman No, not at all. But, actually, I'm not really sure what the problem is. Take this one here – it falls about 125 millimetres in 10.12 metres. And that one – that falls about 75 millimetres in 6.76 metres.

Peter Yes, well in fact that's only about 1 in 90 in each case, you see. I've found that asphalt laid at that fall can result in ponding.

Norman Can it? Hmm – yes, you could be right there.

Peter Of course, I'm not saying it will cause a leak, but I do like to see a flat roof that drains off properly.

Norman Oh yes, I agree entirely with that. And of course, it's particularly important in this case – the roof will be seen from above, won't it?

Peter Oh, so it will. Do you know, I hadn't even thought of that.

Norman Oh yes. Well, I'm very glad you brought up the point. I'll increase the falls to about 1 in 75, then.

Peter Yes, that should be fine.

Norman Good. And I'll amend the drawing and reissue it to you next week.

amend correct, alter
asphalt *see* 3.5.a
cause bring about, produce
care be concerned
drain get rid of water
entirely completely
fall *see* 3.5.c **roof fall**
increase make bigger
indicate show

leak place where water comes through where it shouldn't
particularly especially
personally my own view is
ponding water collecting in a pool or puddle
reissue give out again
result in cause, produce

Answer the questions.

1 Where are the falls Peter is talking about?
2 How would Peter like to see the roof falls changed?
3 What is the approximate gradient of the roof?
4 Why does Peter think the falls should be greater?
5 Why is it especially important for these roofs to drain off properly?
6 What does Norman intend to do?

Complete the minutes of the site meeting (see 0.2).

The site agent suggested ....
He said he had found that ....
The architect agreed that .... and said he thought it was especially important to have good drainage in this case because
.... He said he would .... and
.... next week.

3.2.b Position of Adverbs

Look at these sentences from the conversation:

A   *Personally*, I'd like to see greater falls on here.
    Actually, I'm not really sure what the problem is.

B   It's *particularly* important in this case.
    I'm *very* glad you brought up the point.

Using adverbs adds colour and strength to what we are saying. Adverbs can have different positions in the sentence, and it is important to put them in the right place if their full meaning is to come over. In A above, the adverb, placed first, emphasises the speaker's personal viewpoint. In B, the adverb comes before the adjective, and shows the degree of the adjective.

How important is it? *Particularly* important.
How glad am I? *Very* glad.
Try putting the adverbs in the right place in these sentences:

Example:
Jack is annoyed about the mistakes the bricklayers made. (rather)
Jack is rather annoyed about the mistakes the bricklayers made.

---

1 I prefer pitched roofs to flat ones. (personally)
2 They're interested in these roof-tiles. (particularly)
3 Peter would like to see greater falls. (considerably)
4 They won't have this finished on time. (obviously)
5 I'm certain we shouldn't lay the bricks frog down. (absolutely)
6 In windy weather construction work is dangerous. (extremely)

3.3.a Pitched Roof

'Time is money'
During the erection of a building, many arguments take place over money. The contractor wishes to receive enough to ensure him a profit, and the client wishes to spend no more than his budget sum.

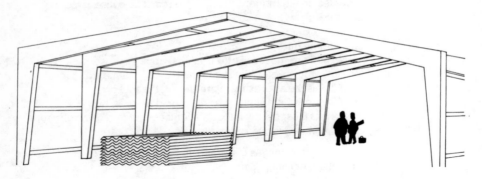

fig 49

Jeff – *Site Surveyor*   Martin – *Consultant Quantity Surveyor*

Jeff You know, we shall need to do a lot of extra work on that profiled steel roofing to the factory. The Bill of Quantities clearly says that no cutting of the sheets is required, doesn't it?

Martin Yes, that's right. Actually, I'm pretty sure the architect designed the portal frame to fit exactly three of those sheets.

Jeff Well, I'm afraid he got it wrong. Two sheets are not far off the right size. And we'll have to cut just under half a sheet length to make up the difference.

Martin Oh? Well, that's funny. You're sure you bought the right product?

Jeff Absolutely positive. Only I've just found out that the manufacturer changed his sheet sizes last year, so now they come a bit longer, you see.

Martin Oh no!

Jeff Yes, I'm afraid so. It's going to mean a lot of extra work, you know. We shall want paying for all this cutting.

Martin Well, I'm not at all sure you'll have to do any. After all, you could probably get sheets the right size from another company, couldn't you?

Jeff Well, I don't know about that. I think it's a bit late now. We ordered the ones in the Bill, and they were delivered yesterday, you see.

Martin Well, the drawing does specify the actual size of sheet, so that means you've either bought the wrong product or else they've sent you the wrong one.

Jeff But you specified a product which isn't made any more!

Martin Hmm – I suppose you're right. But actually, I'm sure the architect will want them changed. Er – perhaps we could agree to share the handling charge?

argument disagreement
Bill of Quantities see Unit Zero
budget sum amount of money a client sets aside to pay for the building
client person or organisation for whom the building is being built
company firm, business organisation
erection putting up
handling charge fee charged by the manufacturer when his product is returned after despatch
manufacturer maker of products
portal frame see fig. 43
profiled steel roofing see 3.6.a
profiled sheet
profit gain
require need
share each pay half

Answer the questions.

1 Why will the contractor have to do a lot of extra work on the profiled steel roofing?

2 How many sheets did the architect intend to use? What does the Bill of Quantities say?

3 Why will it be necessary to do any cutting?

4 Why does Jeff think it would be too late to get the right-sized sheets from another company?

5 What does Martin think the architect will want them to do?

6 Who is going to share the handling charge?

Complete Jeff's part in this conversation in which he is explaining the situation to Norman, the architect.

Norman And what was the problem with the profiled steel roofing?

Jeff ....

Norman But surely not! I designed the portal frame to fit three sheets exactly.

Jeff ....

Norman Well, I don't think you can have bought the right product.

Jeff ....

Norman Oh dear, that does make things difficult. I think you'll have to get the right-sized sheets from another company instead.

Jeff ....

Norman Well, I'm afraid you'll just have to send them back. Otherwise it won't look right at all.

Jeff ....

Norman All right, if the quantity surveyor suggested doing that, it's quite okay by me.

3.3.b 'Want' and 'Need'

'Want' and 'need' have some special uses.

Look at these sentences from the conversation:

A   We shall want paying for all this cutting.

B   The architect will want them changed.

In A the word 'paying' means the same as the passive infinitive ('to be paid'). In other words, the meaning is 'We shall want *to be paid* for all this cutting'.

In B, where there is a direct object ('them'), the word 'changed' again means the same as the passive infinitive, so the meaning of the sentence is 'The architect will want them *to be changed'*.

Both these constructions are common in spoken English, and they can both be used with the verb 'to need' as well as 'to want'.

These sheets need changing, you know.

You'll need that firmly fixed before you carry on.

However, it is more common to use the B construction with 'to want'. Practise using the A construction in the exercise. Answer the question, beginning with 'to need' and using the words in brackets ( ) to complete the sentence.

Example:

When should this roof be finished? (By the end of next week)

It needs finishing by the end of next week.

---

1 How should this sheeting be fixed? (With special bolts)

2 Why should these falls be increased? (So the roof drains off properly)

3 When should these reports be written out? (In time for the next site meeting)

4 Why should we send back this sheeting? (Because it's the wrong size)

5 When should the asphalt be laid? (After the sheathing layer is put down)

6 Why should those tiles be stripped back? (So the party walls can be taken down a bit)

Now change each sentence into a B type like this, beginning with 'Peter wants' each time.

It needs finishing by the end of next week.

Peter wants it finished by the end of next week.

Communication on Site

Giving reasons and opinions and how to show certainty/uncertainty and agreement/disagreement

3.4.a Reasons

On site we often have to give reasons for our actions or intended actions. We sometimes have to find out why things have happened, or explain why to other people, especially when things go wrong. We sometimes give reasons in answer to 'Why . . . ?', 'Why is it that . . . ?', 'How is it that . . . ?' or 'How come . . . ?', although reasons are often given without any questions being asked. In conversation, reasons often start with 'Well, . . .' or 'Well, you see . . .'.

Look at these four answers to the question 'Why do you think the roof falls need increasing?'

   1 Well, you see, asphalt laid at this fall results in ponding. (Fact)

   2 Well, in my experience, asphalt laid at this fall can result in ponding. (Experience)

   3 Well, it's obvious that asphalt laid at this fall will result in ponding. (Conclusion)

   4 Well, you see, it's possible that asphalt laid at this fall could result in ponding. (Possibility)

Look through the three conversations for examples of the different types of reason (fact, experience, conclusion or possibility). Practise giving reasons yourself in answer to the following questions. Make up a reason of the type stated in brackets ( ), and use the three conversations as a basis for your answers.

Example:

Tiler Why do you think this roof is sagging in the middle? (Conclusion)

Jack *Well, it's obvious that the party walls have been taken up too far.*

---

1 **Martin** Why is it that these roof sheets are all the wrong length? (Fact)

   Jeff ....

2 **Mark** Why do you want us to check over all the party walls? (Possibility)

   Jack ....

3 **Peter** Why do you think it's so important for these roofs to drain off properly? (Fact)

   Norman ....

   Martin How come you'll have a lot of extra work to do on the roofing? (Conclusion)

   Jeff ....

5 **Tiler** Why do you think this roof is sagging in the middle? (Possibility)

   Jack ....

6 **Tiler** Why do you think these roof trusses are starting to drop? (Experience)

   Peter ....

3.4.b Opinions

Opinions, like reasons, can be given to back up your decisions and actions. (Opinions are based on personal preference or belief, whereas reasons are based on facts.) Here are some phrases we use to introduce our opinions in English. Notice again we often start with 'Well'.

> To my mind . . .
> Well, I must say, I do like . . .
> If you ask me . . .
> Well, in my view . . .
> I really prefer . . .
> Of course, I would say . . .
> In fact, I think . . .
> Well, in my opinion . . .
> Well, if you want my opinion . . .

There is also a group of adverbs which, when placed first in the sentence, can be used to introduce the speaker's point of view. (See 3.2.b) These include:

Preferably
Actually
Personally
Really
Surely

} These can also be combined with some of the other longer phrases given already.

Practise giving opinions by answering these questions. Base your answers on the three conversations.

Example:
Chief Foreman What do you think of the work the bricklayers have done?
Peter *Well, if you want my opinion, I'd say Jack ought to give them a few lessons.*

---

1 **Norman** What did you want to say about these roof falls?
  Peter ....
2 **Jeff** Well, what do you think we ought to do about this roofing, then, seeing as the sheets are the wrong size?
  Martin ....
3 **Norman** You're not saying a flat roof with this gradient would cause a leak at all, are you?
  Peter ....
4 **Jack** So you think those party walls have been taken up too high, then?
  Peter ....

3.4.c Reasons for opinions

Sometimes opinions are backed up by reasons. Look at this conversation:
Norman What did you want to say about those roof falls?
Peter Well, actually, I really think they ought to be increased a bit.
Norman Oh? And why do you think that?
Peter Well, you see, I've found that asphalt laid at that fall can result in ponding.
Norman Oh, I see.

Write conversations based on this pattern in these situations:

1 The party walls have been taken up too far. (Jack, Peter)

2 The flat roof of the office building needs better drainage. (Peter, Norman)

3 The profiled steel roofing has come in the wrong-sized sheets. (Martin, Jeff)

3.4.d Certainty/ Agreement

When we give reasons and opinions, or listen to other people giving them, it is useful to know how to express certainty/uncertainty and agreement/disagreement.

We can express **certainty** like this:

I'm quite sure . . .

I'm convinced . . .

I'm absolutely certain . . .

There's no doubt . . .

I know for a fact that . . .

and **uncertainty** like this:

Hmm, I don't know . . .

Well, I'm not quite sure . . .

I must say, I have my doubts . . .

Hmm – I think we'd better check on that.

We can express **agreement** like this:

You've got a point there . . .

You could be right there . . .

Yes, I'll go along with that . . .

Oh yes, I agree entirely . . .

Yes, that's exactly what I think . . .

and **disagreement** like this:

Hmm – I'm afraid I don't agree with that.

Well, I suppose you could be right, but . . .

I'm not sure I quite agree with you.

Perhaps you're right, but . . .

Sorry, I can't agree with you.

Look through the three conversations for examples of certainty/uncertainty and agreement/disagreement. Now practise writing your own conversations.

Words you will need:

parapet wall *see* fig. 26

1 Peter, the site agent, is talking to Norman, the architect. Peter is certain the roof falls on the office building should be increased, but Norman doesn't agree. Peter gives plenty of good reasons but Norman thinks it would cost too much because the parapet wall would have to be built up. He is certain that roof falls of 1 in 85 are quite adequate anyway. Write the conversation between them, putting forward their different points of view. It is up to you to decide who wins in the end!

2 Jeff, the site surveyor, is talking to Martin, the consultant quantity surveyor. Jeff explains how it is that the profiled steel roofing has come in sheets the wrong size, and Martin agrees that they have got the wrong size. Jeff is of the opinion that they will need to be paid for all the cutting they will have to do, but Martin isn't certain that they will need to do any cutting at all, and gives his reasons. Write the conversation between them, including what they decide to do in the end.

3.5 Flat Roofs (27.1)

3.5.a Materials and Components

sheet of aluminium

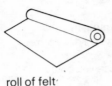

roll of felt

aluminium decking (27.9)Rh4 troughed aluminium sheet for use as roof decking

aluminium foil Th4 aluminium paper used as a vapour barrier

aluminium sheet (47)Mh4 metal roof-covering material

asphalt or mastic asphalt s4 mixture of bitumen and mineral matter occurring naturally

bitumen s1 natural, black, sticky, waterproof material

bituminous felt Ls1 sheet fabric material containing bitumen

copper sheet (47)Mh5 metal roof-covering material, which turns green with age

cork j5 natural insulation material, being the bark of a tree

edge trim (47)Hh metal strip finish to the edge of a roof

expanded polystyrene n7 insulation material formed of white bubbles of plastic foam (soft material containing a lot of air)

foamed phenolic resin n7 type of insulating material in sheet form

fibreboard Rj1 insulating board made from wood fibre

fibreglass insulation material made from glass

lead flat (47)Mh8 sheet of lead used as a roof covering; lead is a soft, grey metal

mineral wool or **mineral fibre** m1 insulation made into a quilt or slab; mineral wool slabs can be built into a cavity wall

rooflight (37.4) window for use in a flat roof

roof outlet (37.9) fitting at the top of a rainwater pipe in a flat roof

sheet of copper

edge trim

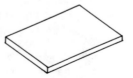

sheet or slab of expanded polystyrene or phenolic foam

a board

fibreglass or mineral wool quilt

mineral wool slab

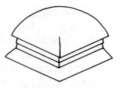

domed rooflight

roof outlet

roof ventilator

roof ventilator (37.9) device fixed on a flat roof to let air into the roof decking or to dry out the roof screed
steel decking (27.9)Rh troughed steel sheet for use as roof decking
stone chippings (47)Ye small pieces of stone to protect a felt roof from sunlight
zinc sheet (47)Mh7 metal roof-covering material

3.5.b Actions

spreading

dressing (D4) forming, pushing into shape, eg dressing asphalt up around a roof ventilator; dressing sheet lead into a brick joint
forming (D4) making, eg forming a drip in a copper-covered roof; forming a joint in a zinc-covered roof
laying asphalt s4(D6) the process of putting asphalt on a roof
spreading asphalt s4(D6) pushing asphalt across a roof to form a thin layer

3.5.c General

angle fillet

angle fillet Hi1 timber fillet used at the edge of a roof where the roof covering is turned up
asphalt apron s4 area of asphalt turned down at the edge of a roof; see fig. 50
bay area of asphalt laid from one batch
blistering bubbles formed in a roof by the heat of the sun
built-up felt roofing (37.9)Ls1 roof covering of several layers of bituminous felt bonded together
coat layer applied at one time, eg two-coat asphalt roofing
cockling lifting up of a roof covering owing to moisture or heat
decking (27.9)R sheet material laid across roof beams or joists to support the roof covering
double lock cross welt Zh welted joint used in metal roofing
drip Zh joint formed in sheet metal roofing
firrings Hi1 pieces of timber fixed to the top of roof joists to provide roof falls
freestanding kerb Hi2 kind of angle fillet; see fig. 50
insulation material which heat cannot pass through quickly
lightweight screed (27)Pq insulating roof screed containing air and light aggregates
minimum fall the smallest slope on a roof which will drain it properly
movement joint Z joint in metal roofing which allows movement caused by heat

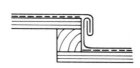
double lock cross welt

drip

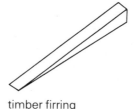
timber firring

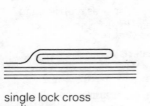

single lock cross welt

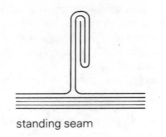

standing seam

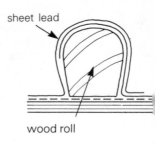

sheet lead

wood roll

roof fall slight slope on a flat roof so that water will run off

roof screed (27)Pq sand/cement mix laid on roof decking, often laid to falls

sheathing felt (27.9)Ls1 layer of bituminous felt laid between asphalt roofing and roof decking; see fig. 50

single lock welt Zh welted joint used in metal roofing

skirting Ps4 area of asphalt turned up a wall; see fig. 50

splayed chase groove cut in brickwork to dress asphalt into; see fig. 50

standing seam Zh joint used in metal roofing

upstand ridge, eg asphalt upstand; see fig. 50

vapour barrier L layer of material to stop moisture from passing through; often included in a flat roof

water check Ps4 asphalt upstand at the edge of a roof; see fig. 50

welted joint Zh joint in metal roofing, eg see **single lock welt**

wood roll Hi2 batten of wood used in batten roll joint in metal roofing

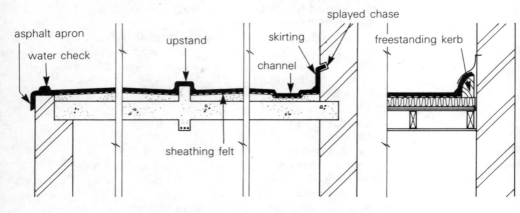

fig 50 Section through asphalt roofing

3.6 Pitched Roofs
(27.2)

3.6.a Materials and Components

asbestos cement f6 hard brittle (easily broken) cement containing asbestos fibres

asbestos cement profiled sheet (47)Nf6 sheet used overlapped on pitched roofs

asbestos cement slate (47)Nf6 roof tile with the appearance of slate

bold roll tile (47)Nf2 concrete tile; see fig. 52

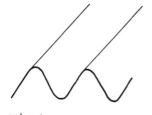

asbestos cement
profiled sheet

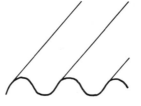

corrugated sheet

driving screw

corrugated sheet (47)N profiled (shaped) roofing sheet made from asbestos cement, steel or transparent plastic

double roman tile (47)Nf2 single lap tile; see fig. 52

driving screw t6 screw driven home with a hammer

eaves filler piece n7 shaped foam packing for profiled sheets

hook bolt t6 steel rod to fix roofing sheet to a steel purlin

interlocking roof tile (47)N clay or concrete single lap tile; see fig. 52

Italian tiles (47)Ng2 single lap tiles; see fig. 51

nail t6 normal fixing for roof tiles

non-ferrous metal h metal containing no iron (chemical symbol Fe)

pan tile (47)N clay or concrete single lap tile; see fig. 51

plain tile (47)N double lap tile; see fig. 51

profiled sheet (47)N shaped sheet, eg corrugated, troughed

ridge finial (47) trim at the end of a ridge

ridge tile (47)N tile fixed along the top of a roof

roof tile (47)N small overlapping roof covering component; see fig. 51

roof window (37.4) window fixed in a pitched roof

shingle Ni1 timber overlapping tile, often made of Red Cedar wood

slate e5 1. kind of stone which easily splits into sheets

slate (47)Ne5 2. flat roof tile made from natural slate

Spanish tiles (47)Ng2 single lap tiles; see fig. 51

steel angle purlin (27)Hh steel angle to which roofing sheets are fixed

troughed sheet R kind of profiled sheet

eaves filler piece

nails

ridge finial

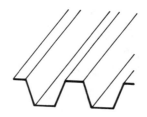

troughed sheet

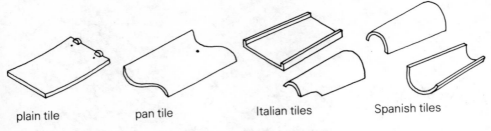

plain tile   pan tile   Italian tiles   Spanish tiles

fig 51 Roof tiles (double lap)

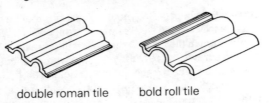

double roman tile   bold roll tile

fig 52 Roof tiles (interlocking)

3.6.b Tools
carborundum saw (B9) see fig. 53
hammer (B7) see fig. 53
mechanical hoist (B9) see fig. 23
pick hammer(B7) slater's hammer; see fig. 53
ripper (B7) slater's tool for removing old slate nails; see fig. 53
rotary cut-off machine (B9) electric power cutter for tiles, bricks,
    stone
scaffold crane (B9) see fig. 53
slate cutter (B7) hand tool; see fig. 53

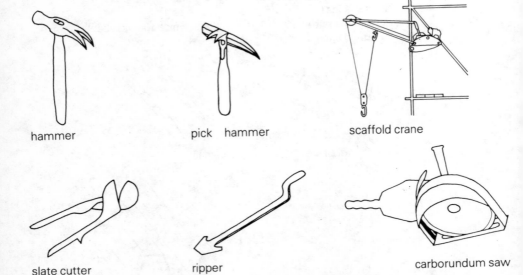

hammer   pick   hammer   scaffold crane

slate cutter   ripper   carborundum saw

fig 53 Tools and plant for roof tiling and slating

cutting (D4) removing part of a roof tile or roofing sheet
driving a nail home (D9) hammering a nail into place
holing a slate (D4) making a hole in a slate
nailing (D9) fixing using nails
slating (D9) fixing slates to a roof
tiling (D9) fixing tiles to a roof

abutment join of a pitched roof with a wall; see fig. 54
barge board (47)i2 board below the verge of a roof; see fig. 54
binder (27.2)i1 hanger
birdsmouth cut made in a rafter
ceiling joist (27)i1 see fig. 55
collar (27.2)i1 see fig. 55
counter battens (47)Hi1 battens to which other battens are nailed at right angles
course (of tiling) one horizontal line of roof tiles; see fig. 59
dormer window (37.4) window set in a pitched roof
eaves bottom edge of a pitched roof
fascia board (47)i2 board fixed along the eaves of a roof; see fig. 55
flashing (47) sheet material, usually metal, used to keep water out at edges of roofs
gable end wall of a pitched roof
gauge measurement of tile spacing; see fig. 59
hanger (27.2)i1 see fig. 55
hip see fig. 54
hip rafter (27.2)i1 see fig. 54
lap measurement of tile overlap; see fig. 59
margin measurement of exposed part of tile; see fig. 59
mansard roof (27.2) roof with two pitches

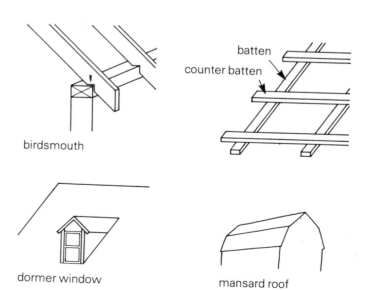

birdsmouth

batten
counter batten

dormer window   mansard roof

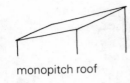

monopitch roof

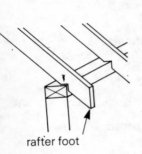

rafter foot

monopitch roof (27.2) roof pitched one side only
open gutter type of gutter formed at the edge of a pitched roof; see fig. 57
pitch the slope of a roof, eg 22.5° pitch; 45° pitch
purlin (27)il see fig. 55
purlin spacing distance between purlins
rafter (27.2)il sloping part in a pitched roof; see fig. 55
rafter foot bottom end of a rafter
random slates (47)Ne5 slates of various sizes, usually laid in diminishing courses, ie the smallest slates at the top of the roof
ridge the top edge of a pitched roof; see fig. 54
sarking (27.9)L waterproof underfelt
secret gutter type of gutter at the edge of a pitched roof; see fig. 57
side lap measure of overlap at the side of a roofing sheet; see fig. 59
soaker (47)Mh8 sheet of lead flashing laid between roof tiles at an abutment
soffit (e) underside, eg of a roof overhang; see fig 55
span distance between supports; see fig. 55
sprocket (27.2)il see fig. 55
strut (27.2)il see fig. 55
translucent see 4.6
transparent see 4.6
tie (27.2)il see fig. 55

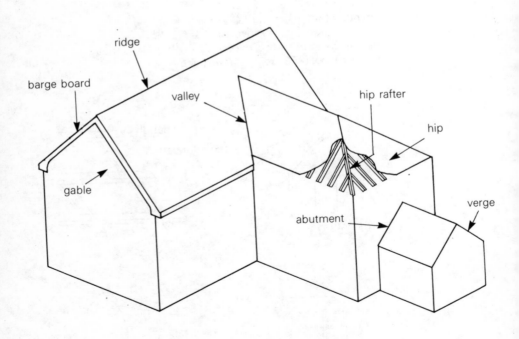

fig 54 Pitched roof

tiling batten (47)Hi1 timber batten to which roof tiles are nailed

tilting fillet (27.2)il see fig. 55

truss (27.9) assembly of structural roof members, which may be prefabricated; see fig. 46

undercloak see fig. 56

underfelt (27.9)L waterproof sheet laid below roofing tiles or slates

valley see fig. 54, 58

verge the edge of a pitched roof; see fig. 54

wall plate length of timber at the top of a wall which rafters rest on; see fig. 55

waste material cut from a building product, which is too small to be of any use

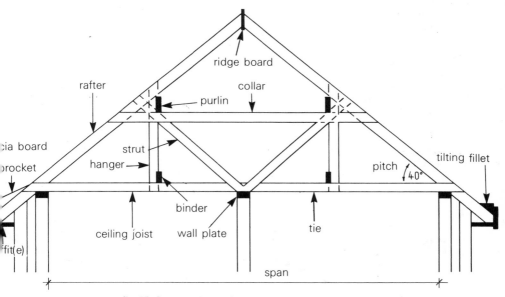

batten

fig 55 **Section through a timber roof**

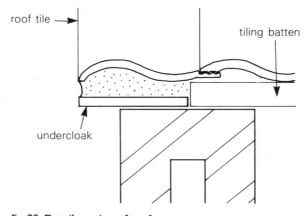

fig 56 **Detail section of roof verge**

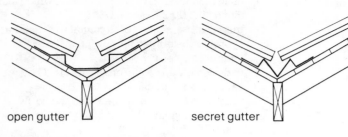

open gutter   secret gutter

fig 57 Roof gutters (detail sections)

fig 58 Roof valleys

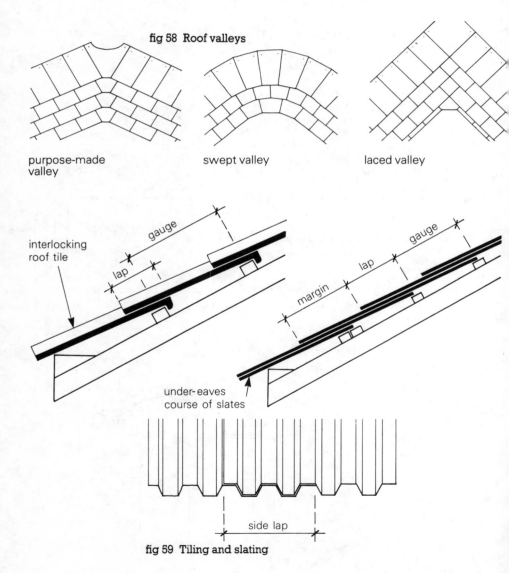

purpose-made valley

swept valley

laced valley

interlocking roof tile

gauge

lap

gauge

lap

margin

under-eaves course of slates

side lap

fig 59 Tiling and slating

3.7 Drawings and Specifications (A3t)

3.7.a Drawings **Plan of a flat roof**

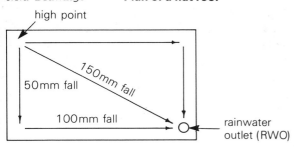

3.7.b Symbols

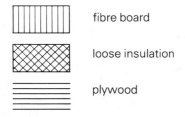

fibre board

loose insulation

plywood

4 Cladding, Glazing and Scaffolding

Language Practice

4.1.a Curtain Wall

'Good organisation depends upon communication'
A specialist sub-contractor must usually carry out his work on site just when needed so that he does not cause delay. This requires careful planning in advance at a site meeting.

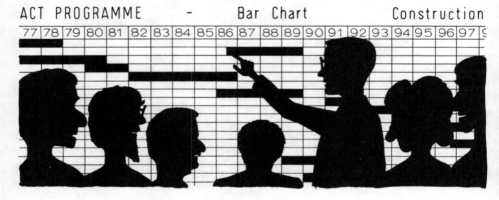

ACT PROGRAMME - Bar Chart Construction

| 77 | 78 | 79 | 80 | 81 | 82 | 83 | 84 | 85 | 86 | 87 | 88 | 89 | 90 | 91 | 92 | 93 | 94 | 95 | 96 | 97 |

fig 60

Peter – *Site Agent*   Mr Hale – *Curtain Walling Sub-contractor*

Peter Right, Mr Hale, so we'll be ready for you to come on site in about two months' time. Let's see – that's week 85, I think.

Mr Hale Hmm – that's about three weeks later than we agreed before, isn't it? But I think we should probably be able to fit in, give or take a few days, of course.

Peter Oh, good. And – er – how long do you expect to be on site?

Mr Hale Well, let's see. The first stage is fixing the mullions. Now that can be tricky because they have to be very carefully aligned.

Peter Oh yes?

Mr Hale Yes, you see the connectors are anchored to each floor, and they have to be adjusted in three directions.

Peter So it's quite a long job, then?

Mr Hale Hmm – I should think it would take about eight working days.

Peter Okay – say two weeks then. And will you need any scaffolding at this stage?

Mr Hale Oh, not necessarily, no. And we can fix the transoms from the inside too. Er – that should only take about three days.

Peter Well, let's see, then – when will you be needing scaffolding?

Mr Hale Oh, I would think after about the middle of week 87 – at the earliest, that is. We need it when we start on the windows.

Peter I see. That's in about ten or eleven weeks, then.

Mr Hale Yes, that's about it. And fixing the windows and spandrel panels – hmm – that'll take two weeks, I would say.

Peter Well, let me know if you think you'll be needing any special equipment, won't you?

Mr Hale Yes. But I can't think of anything at the moment.

adjust set to the correct position
align line up, put in position
anchor fix securely
connector piece joining two parts
curtain wall see 4.5.c
equipment tools, machinery, clothing needed to do a job

fit in do the work at the right time
mullion see 4.5.c
scaffolding see 4.7
spandrel panel see 4.5.c
sub-contractor see 0.1
transom see 4.5.c
tricky difficult

Answer the questions.
1 What work is Mr Hale going to do on site?
2 Why will he be starting work about three weeks later than he thought?
3 How are the mullions aligned? How long does this take?
4 What is the second stage of fixing the curtain walling?
5 Why won't the scaffolding be needed for fixing the transoms?
6 What will the scaffolding be needed for?

Imagine you are Mr Hale and answer these questions asked by Peter.
1 Will it be all right for you to start in about two months' time?
2 What are the different jobs you will have to do?
3 About how long will you be working on each of these?
4 Will you be needing scaffolding from the start?
5 At what stage will you be needing the scaffolding?
6 Will you be needing any special equipment?

4.1.b Time Expressions

Look at these sentences from the conversation:
A We'll be ready for you to come on site in *about two months' time*.
B 'I would think it would take *about eight working days*.
In A, the phrase in *italics* answers the question 'when?'. It tells us at what point in time something is going to happen. In B, the phrase in *italics* answers the question 'how long (will it take)?'. This tells us about a period of time instead of a point in time.

Look through the conversation for other examples of the two types of time expression. Do this exercise to practise using words for 'when?' situations and 'how long (will it take)?' situations:

Example:

Fix the windows: 2 weeks

A   When will you be fixing the windows?
    – In two weeks' time.
B   How long will it take to fix the windows?
    – It'll take two weeks.

1 Do the work	(4 to 5 weeks)
2 Align the mullions	(8 days)
3 Put up the scaffolding	(about 5 days)
4 Fix the transoms	(less than a week)
5 Finish the first stage	(a month or so)
6 Check the fittings	(a few days)

4.2.a Cladding Panels

'A question of tolerance'

Building products cannot always be manufactured to exact sizes, but they must not be too big or too small. The architect specifies the nominal size in his design, but the actual size may be slightly different. The plus (+) or minus (−) inaccuracy allowed is called the tolerance.

fig 61

Peter – *Site Agent*   Mr Taylor – *Manufacturer's Representative*

Peter All these panels have been just the right size until now. So we didn't bother to check this one before it was fixed. But look at that – you can see it's the wrong size, can't you?

Mr Taylor Hmm. Well, the permitted tolerance is plus or minus 3 millimetres. Do you know how far out this one is?

Peter It's about – let's see, now – 5 millimetres too small.

Mr Taylor Oh, well that's nothing to worry about. It's only a little bit out. I don't expect that'll make much difference.

Peter Well, I'm not very happy about it. You see, it could mean a mastic joint of over 15 millimetres wide.

Mr Taylor That's not likely to cause problems, is it?

74

Peter Hmm – I'm not so sure. It's possible for the mastic to fall out, you know. And in any case, a wide joint wouldn't look right. I don't think the architect would be very happy about it either.

Mr Taylor Well, we could supply you with an extra large panel to go next to this one, if you like.

Peter No, it's too late now. All the panels have been delivered already.

Mr Taylor That's a pity. Well, I suppose I'd better get a replacement made as soon as possible, then.

bother take time, make an effort
cladding panel see 4.5.a
mastic see 4.5.a
permit allow

replacement new part to be used in place of a faulty one
tolerance see 4.5.c
worry be concerned

Answer the questions.

1 Why didn't Peter bother to check the problem panel before it was fixed?

2 What is wrong with it?

3 What does Mr Taylor think they should do?

4 Why doesn't Peter want a wide mastic joint?

5 What does Mr Taylor suggest instead? Does Peter think this is a good idea?

6 What will Mr Taylor arrange to have done?

Complete the conversation.

Peter Well, I'm afraid we didn't bother to check this one, and we've found ....

Mr Taylor Hmm – yes, it looks a little small. How far out is it?

Peter ....

Mr Taylor Well, that's only 2 mm outside the permitted tolerance ....
....

Peter No, I really don't think we should because ....

Mr Taylor And what problems do you think that might cause?

Peter ....

Mr Taylor Perhaps the architect would accept...

Peter Well, it's a bit late, isn't it, because ....

Mr Taylor Okay . . . well, in that case..

Peter Yes, that'll be the best thing, I think.

4.2.b Expressions of accuracy

Look at the diagram on the next page:
This shows the side of a building where cladding panels are being fixed. Underneath are four cladding panels supplied by the manufacturers to fill the space in the cladding. There is a 12 mm joint between panels fitted on the building.

1 Work out the nominal size of panel, and make statements about each of the four panels using these expressions.

within the permitted tolerance
not within the permitted tolerance
(Panel A, B, C, D is)   outside the permitted tolerance
exactly the right size
just right

dead right
spot on
too big
too small
a bit out

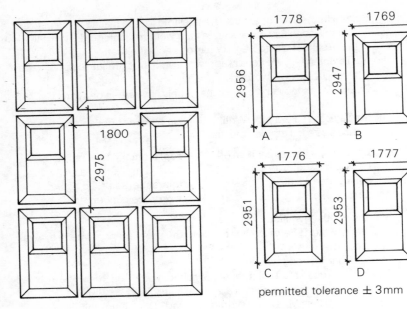

permitted tolerance ± 3 mm

2 Bearing in mind the exact dimensions of the four panels, make as many statements as you can about the accuracy of each panel, using this example to help you.

Panel A, dimension x, is 2 mm outside the permitted tolerance.
Panel A is 5 mm too long.
Panel A is 2 mm more than the nominal width.
Panel A dimension y is 2 mm out.
Panel A is 2 mm too wide.
Panel A is too big in both dimensions.
Panel A dimension y is 1 mm within the permitted tolerance.

3 Answer these questions:

How far out is Panel A, dimension x?
How much out is Panel B, dimension y?
Which panel fits exactly?
Why won't the site agent accept Panels A and B?
Why is he willing to accept Panel D?

4.3.a Scaffolding

'Better safe than sorry'

Building work is dangerous and men are regularly killed or injured on building sites. High standards of safety are necessary to reduce the risk of accidents.

Mr Hamilton – *Safety Officer*   Dick – *Foreman Scaffolder*

Mr Hamilton Hmm – this looks generally safe enough. But I think I'd really like to see a bit more attention to detail with such a high scaffolding.

Dick Well, I've checked it all over; you know, it seemed pretty stable to me – is there anything you're not happy about?

Mr Hamilton Well, for one thing you've missed off all the sole plates under the vertical poles.

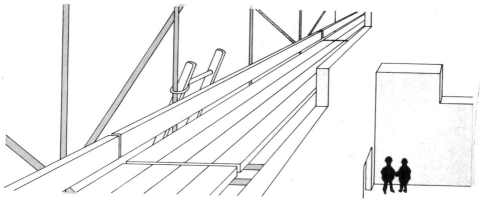

fig 62

Dick Ah, yes – I know that. But I didn't think they'd be needed at all on this firm ground.

Mr Hamilton Hmm – well, even so it's best to put them in, to my mind. It's less likely there'll be any mistakes that way. I usually only allow them to be left off on concrete.

Dick You don't want us to put them in now, do you? We'd have to take the lot down.

Mr Hamilton No, I think we'll leave it as it is now. The ground does seem really firm here, as you say. There shouldn't be any risk.

Dick That's all right then. And are you satisfied with everything else – the general stability, I mean, and the way we've arranged the boards?

Mr Hamilton Yes that's fine. The boards are all level and they seem quite safe. And there seems to be enough bracing to make it all stable. But why have you gone and used two different types of coupler?

Dick Oh, well I'm afraid we didn't have enough of the new ones. I must say, though, I think it's better to use only one type – then there's no confusion.

Mr Hamilton Hmm – well, at least they all seem secure enough. But do try to be more consistent in what you're doing. If you're not, then there's more chance someone'll make a mistake, and that could mean a serious accident.

arrange lay down, put down
board *see* 5.5.b
bracing *see* 4.7 **longitudinal brace**
confusion making mistakes, getting mixed up
consistent uniform, doing things the same
coupler *see* 4.7
firm solid, reliable
injure hurt

level flat, straight
reduce lessen, make less
risk likelihood, chance
scaffolding *see* 4.7
secure safe, certain not to give way
sole plate *see* 4.7
stable firmly fixed, firmly established
to my mind in my opinion
vertical upright

Answer the questions.

1 Why does Mr Hamilton want to see more attention to detail?
2 What does Dick think about using sole plates with this scaffolding?
3 Why does Mr Hamilton think the sole plates should be used?
4 What else is Mr Hamilton not happy about?
5 Why did Dick use two types of coupler?
6 Why does Mr Hamilton think it is important to be consistent?

Fill in the blanks.

Mr Hamilton thought the scaffolding was safe but ....
.... Dick said he'd missed off the sole plates because ....
.... Mr Hamilton didn't think it would be necessary
to put the sole plates on afterwards because ....
.... He was quite satisfied with ....
but .... Dick said he preferred using
only one type of coupler because ....

4.3.b Expressions of safety

Safety is a very important aspect of building work. Safety officers
make regular inspections, yet accidents still happen. Some of the
most serious accidents are falls. Men can fall from ladders,
scaffolding, working platforms, roofs and openings in buildings under
construction. Accidents can be caused by falling materials too. Using
machinery can be dangerous, and men are at risk if they do not use
the correct protective clothing. Every site must have first-aid
facilities. (See 1.5)

helmet

dust mask

safety footwear

protective gloves

goggles

ear protectors

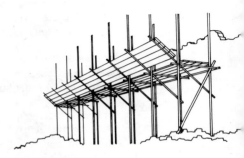
catchment platform

fig 63

Fill in the blanks in this passage with the correct words chosen from below.

Safety precautions recommended on British building sites:
The feet of a ladder should be . . . . . and on . . . . . ground. The top should be . . . . . fixed. On a working platform or roof the open sides should have . . . . . and . . . . . , and tools and materials must be handled . . . . . . Special . . . . . are needed during demolition to avoid falling debris. The danger of . . . . . from machinery becomes more likely as construction work becomes more mechanised. Every . . . . . part of a machine should be properly guarded, and vehicles and machinery should be frequently . . . . . and kept in good working order. The correct . . . . . should always be worn. . . . . . should be used by men working under scaffolding, and safety footwear should be worn for general . . . . . on site.

carefully	protection
checked	protective clothing
dangerous	precautions
firm	safety helmets
guard rails (*see* 4.7)	securely
injury	toe-boards (*see* 4.7)
level	

Communication on Site

Statements about the future: estimation, prediction, possibility and speculation

4.4.a Estimation

Good organisation on site demands constant planning ahead. Even when we are not actually planning, we are often thinking ahead to the next job to be done – when we are going to start it, what we are going to need and so on. In thinking ahead we often need to estimate how much something is going to cost, how much of a product will be needed, how long a particular process is going to take, or when something is going to be done. An estimate is a fairly accurate guess based on experience and calculation. Since it is not an exact statement, we usually use words like 'about', 'approximately' or 'around' when giving an estimate.
Here are some ways to do it:
Let's see, I should think that'll cost around £800.
We should be starting the next job in about two weeks.
I reckon it'll take at least three more drums to finish this.
I expect we'll be about another week on that.
By my calculation, I would say we'll have to spend somewhere in the region of £1,500.
Look through conversation 4.1.a for more examples. Now try making estimates yourself in answer to these questions. Use the words in brackets in your answers.

Example:
How much do you reckon it'll cost to keep the scaffolding for an extra couple of weeks? (£75)
Oh, I'd say that'll be somewhere in the region of £75.

1 How many more of these rolls will we need to finish the job now? (5 more)

2 About how long will the men be working on the roof? (6 days)

3 When will you be able to start fixing the panels? (in 3 days' time)

4 Do you think it will cost a lot to change these scaffold poles for longer ones? (£55)

5 Can you give me any idea how long you'll take to finish off, Mr Hamilton? (3½ working days)

6 About how many more panels will you have to order to do the alterations the architect has made? (15 more)

4.4.b Prediction

An estimate is a kind of prediction, but prediction need not always be connected with cost, quantities and time. On site we make predictions about many other things. Look at these examples:

This job is going to take much longer than we expected.

If those bricks are stacked too near the edge, they'll fall off.

You'd better use sole plates here or I'm sure Mr Hamilton won't pass the scaffolding.

If we don't get this job finished soon, the weather will be too cold for us to carry on.

When they learn to work more consistently there will be fewer mistakes made.

When we are not sure enough of our facts to make predictions, we might instead talk about the probability or possibility of something happening. Look at these expressions ranging from probable to possible:

Probable
I'm pretty sure you'll
I expect you'll
It's quite likely you'll
You'll probably
I should think you'll
I dare say you'll

Possible
Perhaps you'll
It's possible you'll
You might
There's just a chance you'll

} be able to use that cladding panel after all

Look through conversation 4.2.a for examples of probability and possibility. Look back to the examples of prediction above, and change each of the sentences first into a 'probable' sentence and then a 'possible' sentence, using different expressions each time.

Now try to make up two more replies to each of the following questions, using first probability and then possibility.

Example:

Fixer Why do we have to align these mullions so accurately?

Mr Hamilton Well, if they're not done right we won't be able to fit the spandrel panels properly.

(Probability) *Well, if they're not done right it's quite likely we'll have difficulty fitting the spandrel panels properly.*

(Possibility) *Well, if they're not done right I dare say we might find it hard to fit the spandrel panels properly.*

---

1 **Labourer** Why don't you want us to use steel and aluminium poles together on the scaffolding?

   Dick Ah well, you see, steel is much stronger than aluminium, and if you use them together you'll find the aluminium ones will be overloaded.

2 **Fitter** Can't we use this panel, then? It's only just outside the permitted tolerance.

   Peter No, I don't want you to. The mastic joint will be far too big if you do.

3 **Dick** Do you really think we need sole plates here?

   Mr Hamilton Well, I really don't think the ground is firm enough here. The scaffolding won't be safe enough if you leave them off.

4.4.c Speculation

Talking about the probability or possibility of certain things happening is a way of speculating about the future. On site we sometimes speculate about the different ways of solving a problem, or weigh up the advantages and disadvantages of using different methods or materials. Here is a conversation showing ways to speculate.

A If we were to use this panel here, it might mean a mastic joint of over 15 mm wide.

B Yes, but if we sent it back we'd probably have to wait a long time for a replacement.

A Well, suppose we did use it then, it's just possible the mastic might fall out of that joint.

B Hmm, you could be right. Well, say we left this panel for a bit then. We might just find a very large panel we could put beside it later on.

Practise speculating in this exercise. Imagine a situation where Peter is talking to Nick, one of the sheet cladding fixers. One of the sheets, which is specially cut to fit round a window, has been broken and is unusable. They must get another sheet specially cut to fit. They could either do this on site by hand, or they could send a sheet back to the workshop to be cut by machine. There are advantages and disadvantages on both sides. If they did the job on site it would be quite a lot of work and the cutting might not be quite accurate. If they sent a sheet to the workshop it would mean an hour's travelling each way and they would have to use one of the site vehicles which might be needed for something else. Write the conversation between them where they speculate on the two possibilities and eventually decide upon one or the other. Begin like this:

Peter Hey, Nick, you know that special panel's been broken don't you? Do you think we ought to get another one cut on site, or send one back to the workshop to be done?

4.5 Cladding (41)

4.5.a Materials and Components

adjustable corbel plate t6 fixing for stone cladding; see fig. 64
brick F material used in cladding walls and sometimes in precast cladding panels
brick slip or **brick tile** (41)Fg thin brick

 brick

 brick slip

building paper Ls9 paper with a layer of bitumen
ceramic tile (41)Sg3 clay wall tile
cladding panel (21.6)G wall panel made in a factory; the finish may be concrete, brick, glass reinforced plastic (GRP) or glass reinforced cement (GRC)
cladding tile (41)N tile similar to a roofing tile, fixed to a wall
corbel plate Zt6 fixing for stone cladding; see fig. 64
dovetail anchor Zt6 fixing for cladding panels; see fig. 64
epoxy resin glue t3 very strong adhesive which may be used to glue concrete members together
fishtailed cramp t6 fixing for cladding panels; see fig. 64
fixing dowel t6 fixing for cladding panels; see fig. 64
fixing lug t6 fixing for cladding panels; see fig. 64
gasket Zh5 plastic strip used in a joint between two cladding panels; see fig. 67
glass Ro see 4.6
glass reinforced cement (GRC) f2 strong, light cement reinforced with glass fibre, used to make cladding panels
glass reinforced plastic (GRP) n8 strong, light plastic material reinforced with glass fibre, used to make cladding panels
mastic Zh5 substance used for sealing joints
mosaic (41)Sg3 decorative finish of tiny pieces of glazed clay, sometimes used on external walls
profiled metal cladding sheet (21.6)N wall cladding sheet made of aluminium, steel or asbestos cement
render (41)Pq2 smooth cement finish applied with a trowel to a brick or concrete wall
shiplap board (41)Hi2 type of weatherboard

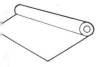
roll of building paper

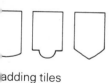
cladding tiles

mosaic

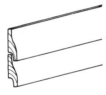
profiled sheets

shiplap boards

weather boards

stone Fe natural building material found in the ground; stone may be cut into thin slabs for use as a cladding material

tie cramp t6 fixing for cladding panels; see fig. 64

vapour barrier sheet or layer which does not allow moisture to pass through it

vitreous enamel v4 glass finish on a metal surface, used on steel cladding panels

weatherboard (41)Hi2 timber cladding board fixed horizontally

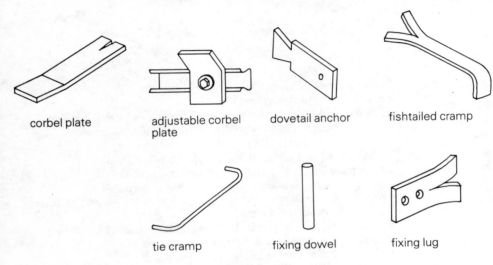

corbel plate

adjustable corbel plate

dovetail anchor

fishtailed cramp

tie cramp

fixing dowel

fixing lug

fig 64 Fixing for cladding panels

4.5.b Tools

hammer (B7) hand tool for driving nails

mastic gun (B7) tool for putting mastic into a joint; the mastic is forced out through a nozzle

spanner (B7) hand tool for tightening bolts

tower crane (B3t) see fig. 9

trowel (B7) tool used to apply sand/cement render

hammer

nozzle

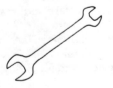

spanner

trowel

4.5.c General

back-up wall (21.4)F an internal wall behind a curtain wall

butt joint Z see fig. 67

composite panel (21.6)G cladding panel made from several materials; see **sandwich panel**

compression joint Z see fig. 67

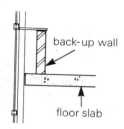

back-up wall

floor slab

curtain wall
(section)

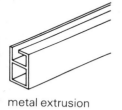

metal extrusion

condensation groove channel to collect water which forms at the back of a cladding panel; see fig. 65

core material (21.6) material in the middle of a sandwich panel

curtain wall (21.4) lightweight wall usually glazed, attached to the structure of a building to keep out the weather

dimensional grid (F7) series of lines through a building which help to plan and construct the building; see 4.8.a

drained joint Z see fig. 67

extrusion H length of plastic or metal made by pushing the material hard through a hole of the right shape; eg metal glazing frames are often made of extruded metal

lap joint Z see fig. 67

locating dowel t9 fixing which helps to get a cladding panel in the right position; see fig. 65

framework (21.4)H the mullions and transoms which form a frame to support a curtain wall

mated joint Z see fig. 67

module (F7) dimension within a dimensional grid; see 4.8.a

mortice hole formed in the back of a piece of stone cladding; see fig. 66

mullion (21.6)H vertical part of a window frame or curtain wall framework

non-ferrous metal metal containing no iron (chemical formula Fe)

opaque (G6) allowing no light to pass through, ie not translucent; eg sheet steel is opaque, but clear glass is not

prefabrication (E3) manufacture of a component before it is fixed on site

rib thickened part of a cladding panel; see fig. 65

sandwich panel (21.6)G cladding panel made of several materials glued together; one of the materials is usually insulation

soffit(e) cladding (41)e stone cladding fixed horizontally; see fig. 66

spandrel panel (21.6)G panel in a curtain wall between one window and the window above or below

tile hanging (41)N clay or concrete tiles fixed vertically

tolerance (F6) dimension by which a building component may be made too big or too small, eg the tolerance for a concrete cladding panel may be plus (+) or minus (−) 4 mm, ie ± 4 mm

translucent (G7) allowing light to pass through, ie not opaque

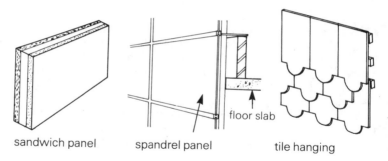

sandwich panel   spandrel panel   tile hanging

floor slab

transom (21.6)H horizontal part of a window frame or curtain wall framework

transparent (G7) able to be seen through, eg clear glass is transparent, but frosted glass is not

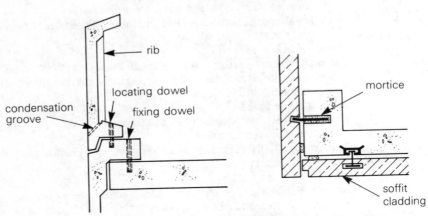

fig 65 Cladding panel (section)

fig 66 Stone cladding (section)

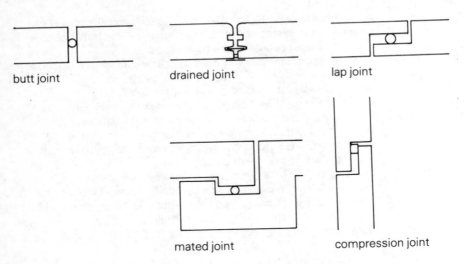

butt joint

drained joint

lap joint

mated joint

compression joint

fig 67 Cladding panel joints (plan details)

4.6 Glazing Ro

diamond wired glass

armourplate glass Ro8 toughened (very strong) glass

diamond wired glass Ro4 glass reinforced with wire; cast quality is not transparent; polished quality is transparent

elastomeric sealant Yu5 good quality material which keeps water out at the edges of sheets of glass, often used in tall buildings

float glass Ro1 good quality smooth, flat glass

frosted glass Ro2 glass which cannot be seen through, suitable for use in a bathroom window

gasket Hu rubber or plastic glazing strip; see fig. 68

Georgian wired glass

glass cutter

reeded glass

Georgian wired glass Ro4 glass reinforced with wire; cast quality is not transparent; polished quality is transparent

glass Ro material most commonly used to let light into buildings; most types are transparent

glass cutter B7 hand tool for cutting glass

glass fin Ro part of a suspended glass structure; see fig. 69

glazing bead H strip which holds glass in a frame; see fig. 68

glazing compound Yy soft material into which sheets of glass are bedded (laid), and which may go hard later; see fig. 68

laminated glass Ro8 strong sheet of glass made up of several sheets of glass and plastic

mirrored glass Ro7 solar control glass

neoprene n5 plastic-like rubber used to stop water from coming into windows

non-setting glazing compound Yy glazing compound which does not go hard

patch fitting Zt6 fixing used in suspended glass; see fig. 69

patent glazing Ro prefabricated system of weatherstripped glazing bars and sheets of glass for glazing large areas

patterned glass Ro2 glass with a shaped surface; patterned glass is not transparent

plate glass Ro1 good quality flat glass

polycarbonate sheet Rn6 very strong transparent material which looks like glass, and is very hard to break

putty Yt4 soft material used to hold glass in a frame; it goes hard later

reeded glass Ro2 type of patterned glass

solar control glass Ro6 glass which does not allow all of the heat and light of the sun to pass through it

wash leather Tj6 soft leather into which sheets of glass are bedded (laid)

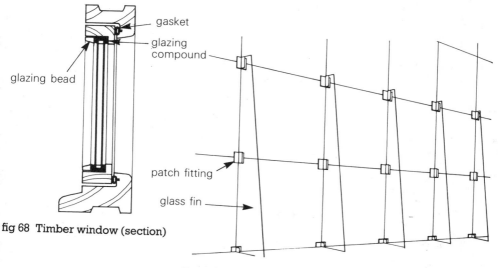

fig 68 Timber window (section)

fig 69 Suspended glass

4.7 Scaffolding (B2d)

base plate

adjustable base plate

castor wheel

swivel coupler

base plate metal plate placed at the bottom of a scaffold pole

bridle horizontal scaffold pole; see fig. 70

castor wheel wheel for use at the bottom of a scaffold tower

coupler device which fixes two scaffold poles together

guard rail scaffold pole fixed horizontally to act as a handrail; see fig. 70

joint pin part used to join two scaffold poles end to end

ladder see fig. 70

lashing rope used to fix the top of a ladder to a scaffold pole

ledger horizontal scaffold pole; see fig. 70

lift distance between one boarded walkway and the next one on a scaffold; see fig. 70

longitudinal brace see fig. 70

pre-coupled unit scaffold pole with couplers welded to it

putlog horizontal scaffold pole supported by a wall at one end; see fig. 70

scaffold board board laid across putlogs

scaffold pole steel or aluminium pole used to form a temporary structure to work from

scaffold tower scaffolding made from units which slot together

sole plate length of timber laid below scaffolding base plates

standard main supporting vertical scaffold pole; see fig. 70

swingover box spanner spanner for tightening couplers

toe board scaffold board laid on its edge at the side of a scaffold walkway; see fig. 70

transom horizontal scaffold pole; see fig. 70

transverse brace see fig. 70

trestle scaffold low scaffold which may be erected quickly

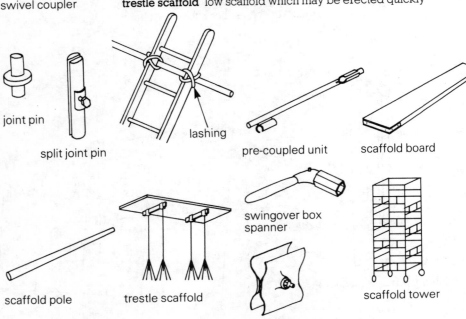

joint pin

split joint pin

lashing

pre-coupled unit

scaffold board

scaffold pole

trestle scaffold

swingover box spanner

lapping coupler

scaffold tower

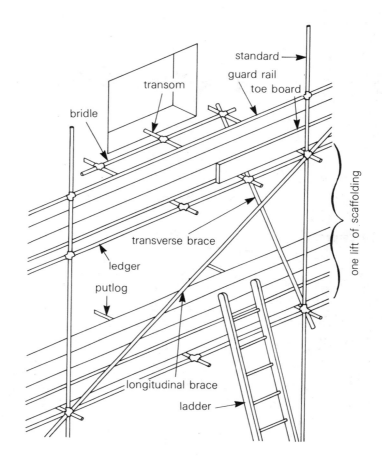

fig 70 Scaffolding

4.8 Drawings and Specifications (A3t)

4.8.a Drawings

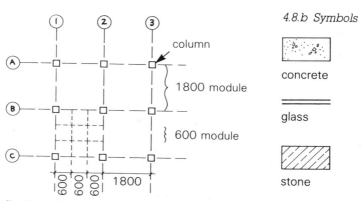

fig 71 Building frame (plan)

4.8.b Symbols

concrete

glass

stone

5   Carpentry and Joinery

Language Practice

5.1.a Carpentry

'We can all make mistakes'
The building design consultants (architects, structural engineers, service engineers) sometimes make mistakes on their drawings. The contractor may notice them, or they may not be noticed until it is too late.

fig 72

Norman – *Architect*   Bill – *Foreman Carpenter*

Bill Well, that's it then. That roof to Block 1 is complete now, as you can see. And Block 2 isn't far behind.

Norman Hmm – these battens they're plugging to the brickwork – they're fixings for the fascia board, aren't they?

Bill Yes, that's right. It's a stained batten, ex. 38 by 38.

Norman But there should be gaps here. They don't seem to be leaving any gaps for air to pass between the roof timbers – look.

Bill Oh dear, I didn't spot that, I'm afraid. But you know, I don't think we've been instructed to do it that way.

Norman Oh? Well, there definitely should have been a note on the drawing. You must know it's essential to allow ventilation to the roof at the eaves.

Bill Yes, I know. I'm sorry I didn't notice it myself. I would have mentioned it to you earlier if I'd spotted it.

Norman Well, never mind. Let's see what we can do about it. You'll have to leave gaps in the battens from now on. I think it'd better be 25 millimetre gaps at 600 millimetre centres, please. That'll be on all the blocks that aren't finished yet – Blocks 2 to 7.

Bill Okay.

Norman We can't do that on Block 1, though. Hmm – I think I'll get you to drill holes there instead. Would you drill 25 millimetre holes at 600 millimetre centres on that one?

Bill Yes, that'll be okay.

Norman And don't forget you should put mouse guards at all the gaps.

batten *see* 5.5.b	**mention** say
carpentry work with timber	**mouse guard** metal fixture to
definitely certainly	prevent mice getting into
drilling *see* 5.5.d	buildings
eaves *see* 3.6.d	**notice** see, catch sight of
essential absolutely necessary	**plugging** *see* 5.5.d
fascia board *see* 3.6.d	**spot** notice, see
gap space	**stained** *see* 6.6.a **wood stain**

Answer the questions.

1 What are the battens made from?
2 What are the gaps in the battens for?
3 Why haven't the carpenters been leaving any gaps?
4 Why didn't Bill mention it to Norman earlier?
5 What will the men do with the battens on Blocks 2 to 7? Why can't they leave gaps on Block 1?
6 Where will the mouse guards be fixed?

Norman is telling another architect what happened on site. Fill in the blanks.

You see, the fixings for the fascia board are ....
If the roof is to be properly ventilated, then, ...
.... The instructions about leaving gaps had been missed off the drawing, so .... Unfortunately the foreman didn't notice, or .... So on Block 1 he had to .... to put it right. On the other blocks the men were able to ....

5.1.b Uses of 'should'

Look at these sentences from the conversation:

There *should have been* a note on the drawing.

There *should be* gaps here.

Don't forget you *should put* mouse guards at all the gaps.

'Should' here expresses obligation or how things ought to be. We can use it with an idea of past ('should have'), present or future, as the three sentences show. Practise using it in the following exercise. Use the past tense of should ('should have') where shown.

Example:

There (be) a note on the drawing.

There should be a note on the drawing.

There (be – *past*) a note on the drawing.

There should have been a note on the drawing.

---

1 The men (leave) gaps for air to pass between the roof timbers.
2 A roof (always – be ventilated) properly at the eaves.
3 We (have – *past*) instructions to leave gaps at 600 mm centres.
4 Bill says he (notice – *past*) the mistake earlier.
5 These mouse guards (be fitted) at all the gaps.
6 Perhaps you (drill) holes on Block 1 instead.

5.2.a Carpentry   *'The Building Inspector calls on site'*

The building inspector visits the site regularly to ensure that the building is being constructed as shown on the approved drawings.

fig 73

Mr Clark – *Building Inspector*   Peter – *Site Agent*

Mr Clark I've just been round the site to see how things are going. Er – I see you've started fixing some of the floor joists in the houses.

Peter Yes, that's right. We had hoped to start before now, but the joist hangers didn't arrive until yesterday.

Mr Clark Well, I'm afraid they'll have to be changed. Those joists are not the same as on the drawings.

Peter Are you sure? Are they too small or something?

Mr Clark Oh no, they're the right size. No, the trouble is, they should be stress-graded timber.

Peter But they are! I know we *ordered* stress-graded timber, and it all arrived a couple of weeks ago. I can show you the order and the delivery note.

Mr Clark Well, I'm sorry, but there are no marks on those joists to show the timbers have been stress graded.

Peter But I saw that timber when it arrived. I just don't understand what's happened.

Mr Clark Well, there's obviously been a mix-up somewhere.

Peter Typical! I suppose those stupid chippies have gone and used it for something else!

Mr Clark You know it'll have to be altered, don't you? I'm sorry it's going to be such a lot of work, but it can't be helped.

Peter All right, I'll see it's put right. And I'll have a thing or two to say to those chippies too.

Mr Clark Er – there was one other thing. You will be using steel herringbone strutting, won't you?

Peter Oh yes. It's in the specification.

Mr Clark Good. I prefer it to timber.

alter change
approved officially accepted
building inspector see 0.1
chippie site word for carpenter.
  See 0.1 **carpenter**
delivery note list of items
  delivered
ensure make sure
floor joists see 5.5.h **joist**
it can't be helped there's no
  other way, it can't be avoided

joist hangers see 5.5.h
mark identifying sign
mix-up misunderstanding,
  mistake
specification see 0.2
steel herringbone strutting see
  5.5.h **herringbone strutting**
stress-graded timber see 5.5.a
typical! as usual!

Answer the questions.

1 Why does the building inspector visit the site?

2 Why did Peter have to wait before they started fixing the floor joists?

3 What is the difference between the joists as specified on the drawing and the joists that have been used in the houses?

4 How does Peter know for sure that the stress-graded timber has been delivered?

5 How does Mr Clark know that the timbers used are not stress graded?

6 What sort of strutting will they be using?

Fill in the blanks in the conversation.

Peter Ah, hello again, Mr Clark. Have you had a good look round now?

Mr Clark ....

Peter Oh yes, now the joist hangers have arrived we've been able to get started on them at last.

Mr Clark ....

Peter Changed? But whatever's wrong with them?

Mr Clark ....

Peter What? But it *must* be stress graded. We had the timber all ready last week. Are you sure?

Mr Clark ....

Peter Well, I just don't understand how it could have happened.

Mr Clark ....

Peter Yes, I suppose you're right. The men must have used the stress-graded timber somewhere else.

Mr Clark ....

Peter Yes, I realise we can't leave it like this. I think I'll go and see the men straight away and get it put right.

5.2.b Using past tenses

Look at these sentences from the conversation:

It all *arrived* a couple of weeks ago.
But I *saw* that timber when it arrived.
The joist hangers *didn't arrive* until yesterday.

In these sentences, using the simple past tense (in *italics*), the action took place in the past. Each sentence contains a phrase telling us something about *when* the action happened.

Now look at some other sentences from the conversation:

I see you've *started* (have started) fixing some of the floor joists.
There's obviously *been* (has been) a mix-up somewhere.
There are no marks to show the timbers *have been stress graded*.
Those stupid chippies *have gone* and *used* it for something else.

In these sentences, using the present perfect tense, there is no information about *when* the action happened.

Use the correct tense in each of the sentences in this exercise.

Example:
I (not see) the timber when it arrived.
I *didn't see* the timber when it arrived.

1 Mr Clark (look round) the site before the joists were fixed.
2 I think the carpenters (use) the wrong timber on these joists.
3 I hope you (not use) stress-graded timber in this door frame as well.
4 We (start) on the joists as soon as the joist hangers were delivered.
5 I (look for) the marks on the timber, but there don't seem to be any.
6 I'll just check over those joists the men (fix) yesterday.

5.3.a Joinery

'*Drawings should be well drawn and well read*'
An important part of learning a skill in building is learning how to understand drawings and read information accurately from them.

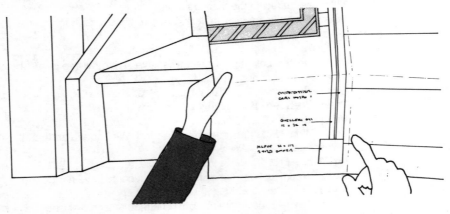

fig 74

Bill – *Foreman Carpenter*   Dennis – *Apprentice Carpenter*

Bill You'll soon have those stairs finished now, Dennis. Let's just see how you're getting on . . . oh, there seems to be something a bit wrong here, I think.

Dennis Yes, I'm not sure what's happened. You see I've tenoned the handrail into the newel post – here, see – but the fixings to the wall don't seem to match up with the drawing – look.

Bill Oh, I see what you've done. It's in the wrong position, isn't it? You can't fix it there, you know. Halfway up the stairs you'll jam your fingers between the handrail and the wall, see.

Dennis Perhaps the wall's been built in the wrong place.

Bill The wrong place? No! Look, you've fixed the *newel post* in the wrong place. Here, look at the drawing again. It should be notched over the string 38 millimetres, you see. That'll make all the difference.

Dennis Oh yes, I see it now. I'm afraid I haven't really got used to reading these drawings yet. Well, I suppose I'd better get this handrail out of the newel post before the glue sets, then.

Bill Oh, don't bother doing that. In fact, you'd better leave it for a couple of hours till after lunch. Then it'll have a chance to set firm. But make sure you loosen the post at the bottom there first. Otherwise that'll set in the wrong position, won't it?

Dennis Okay. But then how will I manage to get the newel post into the right position afterwards?

Bill Well, you'll have to saw it carefully at the bottom there so it'll fit over the string. Then you'll be able to glue it in the proper position. And I'm sure you'll find those handrail fixings will be all right too.

accurate correct, exact
bother take time, make an effort
glue substance for sticking things together, used in joinery for wood joints
handrail *see* 5.5.g
jam catch
joinery the making and fixing of doors, windows and other wooden parts of a building
loosen unfix, free
newel post *see* 5.5.g
notch *see* 5.5.d
proper right, correct
saw *see* 5.5.d
set become hard, become firm
skill job involving accurate use of tools
string *see* 5.5.g
tenon *see* fig. 93

Answer the questions.

1 What problem is Dennis having with the handrail?

2 If he fixes the handrail in the wrong position, what will happen when he goes upstairs?

3 What has Dennis done with the newel post? Where should the newel post be positioned?

4 Why has he made this mistake?

5 What does Bill tell him to do to get the newel post into position?

6 What will Dennis do with the newel post after he has sawn it at the bottom?

Complete the sentences.

1 Dennis has been ....
2 The wall-fixings don't match up with the drawing because ....
3 Dennis didn't realise the newel post should be ....
4 If he doesn't loosen the newel post at the bottom, then ....
5 To make it fit properly he'll have to ....
6 If he gets the newel post in the correct position, then ....

5.3.b Phrases in conversation

There are several words and short phrases used all the time in conversation for joining ideas together, filling in time, or adding extra meaning to what we are saying.
Here are some of them.

Well	(usually linking with previous idea)
So . . . . . then	(coming to a conclusion)
You see	(explaining)
You know	(informing)
In fact	(pointing out the truth)
Tag questions	(*see* 1.1.b)

'Well' and 'so' are used at the beginning of a sentence and can be put together with some of the other phrases for extra meaning. 'You see', 'you know' and 'in fact' can come at the beginning or end of a sentence. Tag questions always come at the end. Look through the conversation to see how some of these phrases are used. Practise them yourself in this exercise, writing Bill's reply to Dennis and using the phrase in brackets ( ) in your answer.

Example:
Dennis You seem to jam your fingers here between the handrail and the wall. (so)
Bill *Oh, so the rail's been fixed too close to the wall then, has it?*

1 **Dennis** What's gone wrong here, Bill? The handrail seems to be too close to the wall. (you see)
2 **Dennis** The newel should be a bit farther over, shouldn't it? (in fact)
3 **Dennis** I'll get this handrail out of the newel post before the glue sets, then. (you know)
4 **Dennis** I'm afraid I couldn't really understand how to fix this properly. (so)
5 **Dennis** And how should I get this newel post into the right position now the handrail's set? (you see)
6 **Dennis** Are you sure those handrail fixings will be right now? (tag question)

Communication on Site

Asking for information and describing things

5.4.a Questions

The most obvious way of getting information is to ask questions using one of the question words, which are:
how? where? what? who? when? why?
You will probably have done more answering than asking questions

in English. Now try doing the asking yourself, putting the right question to get these answers.

Example:
The men must leave gaps in the battens because it is essential to allow ventilation to the eaves. (why?)
Why must the men leave gaps in the battens?

---

1 The carpenters are fixing battens for the fascia board. (what?)
2 The timber all arrived a couple of weeks ago. (when?)
3 We have to use stress-graded timber here because it's in the specification (why?)
4 The newel should be fixed so it is notched 38 mm over the string. (how?)
5 They'll need to put mouse guards at all the gaps. (where?)
6 The post must be loosened at the bottom or it'll set in the wrong position. (why?)

Don't forget there are other ways to use 'how' (how big?, how many?, how much longer? etc) and 'what' (what sort of? what is the matter with? what colour?). There is also the question word 'which?' for choosing alternatives:
Which timber are we using for the joists?
(The stress-graded timber).

5.4.b 'Checking' questions

We often ask questions expecting a yes/no answer, where no question word is needed. Look at these examples from the conversations in this unit:
They're fixings for the fascia board, aren't they?
Are they too small or something?
You will be using steel herringbone strutting, won't you?
(See also 1.1.b 'Tag questions' for more examples.)
These are 'checking' questions rather than asking for any *new* information. The form we use often depends on what we expect for an answer. (Sometimes questions of this type do not even have to be put in question form. We make them into questions by the tone of voice):
Look at these examples. The expected answer is given afterwards.
Isn't this handrail finished, then? Definite No
Is this handrail finished now? Yes/No
This handrail's finished now, is it? Yes (Possible No)
This handrail's finished now, isn't it? Yes
So this handrail's finished, then? Definite Yes
Here are some statements. Make them into 'checking' questions, using a different form each time.

Example:
There are no instructions on the drawing about leaving gaps.
Are there no instructions on the drawing about leaving gaps, then?

---

1 It isn't necessary to allow ventilation to the eaves here.
2 They should have put mouse guards on Blocks 2 to 7.
3 They've started fixing the floor joists in some of the houses now.
4 The joists on Block D aren't stress-graded timber.
5 The newel post has been fixed in the wrong position.
6 That post should be notched over the string 38 millimetres.

5.4.c Describing things

Asking for information is important on site, and so is describing and talking about what we can see. Look at these drawings.

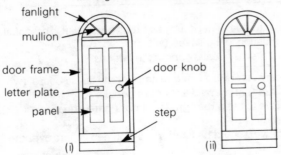

fanlight
mullion
door frame
door knob
letter plate
panel
step
(i)   (ii)

Try to describe in detail what you can see in drawing (i) above, using the words given on the drawing. Describe the shape, size and position of different parts of the door, and what each is made of. Now look at drawing (ii) above, showing the finished door, and describe in detail what is wrong with it.

Now look at the drawings below of an open tread staircase (i) as it was designed and (ii) as it was incorrectly made. Describe as fully as you can what is wrong with the finished staircase.

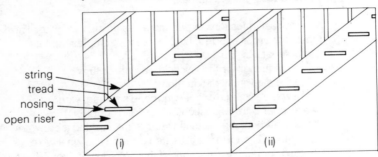

string
tread
nosing
open riser
(i)   (ii)

5.4.d Practice conversation

Look back to the conversation in 5.3.a. Imagine you are Bill, the foreman carpenter, talking to Peter, the site agent, in the lunch break. You are describing to Peter what Dennis did wrong this morning, and how the mistake was put right.

Fill in the blanks in the conversation.

Peter And what did you put Dennis on this morning?

Bill ....

Peter But the drawing shows the newel notched over the string, doesn't it? Didn't he look at the drawing or something?

Bill ....

Peter Oh, well. He's only new yet. I suppose he'll get used to them in time. How did you manage to sort it out then?

Bill ....

Peter I see. So he'll be finishing the job off this afternoon, then?

Bill .....

Peter Yes, I hope they'll be all right too!

5.5 Carpentry and Joinery

5.5.a Materials

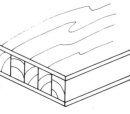

blockboard

broad leaf

blockboard i4 timber sheet made from plywood and strips of softwood

chipboard j7 timber sheet made from particles of wood glued together

fibre board j1 insulating board made from wood fibres

fungicide u3 liquid which kills mould (fungus) which grows on damp surfaces

hardboard j1 dense board made from compressed wood fibres, in 3 grades: standard, tempered and medium

hardwood j3 timber from a tree with a broad leaf

insulation board j1 fibre board

laminboard i4 timber sheet similar to blockboard, but stronger

masonite j1 hardboard

melamine n6 plastic used in thin sheets to cover timber sheet materials; eg kitchen furniture is often faced with melamine

particle board j7 chipboard

plywood j4 laminated timber sheet

preservative u3 liquid which stops wood from going rotten, eg wet rot, dry rot

seasoned timber i timber which has been allowed to dry out over a long period

softwood i2 timber from a tree with a pinnate leaf

stress-graded timber i timber for structural use which has been tested for strength

timber i natural building material measured by the cubic metre; eg a timber-framed building; sawn timber; planed (wrot) timber

wood i timber; eg a piece of wood; a wooden plank; a wood block floor

wood wool j8 material formed into slabs using very thin strips of wood mixed together with cement

laminboard

plywood (3-ply)

pinnate leaf

5.5.b Components

batten Hi strip of wood

bead Hi strip of wood, smaller than a batten

bent Hi piece of wood finished in a curved shape

board Ri hard sheet, usually made from wood

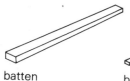
batten

bead

bent

board

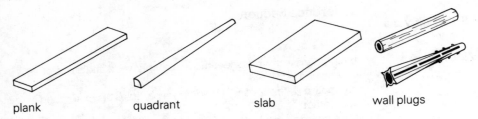

plank   quadrant   slab   wall plugs

length of wood Hi long piece of wood, eg a batten or a bead
nail t6 metal fixing driven into wood with a hammer; see fig. 75
plank Hi narrow board; planed timber is not usually called a plank
quadrant Hi planed bead with a curved face
screw t6 metal fixing screwed into wood with a screwdriver, made of
    steel or brass; see fig. 76
sheet Ri flat piece of material, eg a sheet of plywood
slab Ri thick board
sprig t6 nail without a head; see fig. 75
strip Hi small length of timber
wall plug t6 piece of plastic or wood to hold a wood screw in a wall

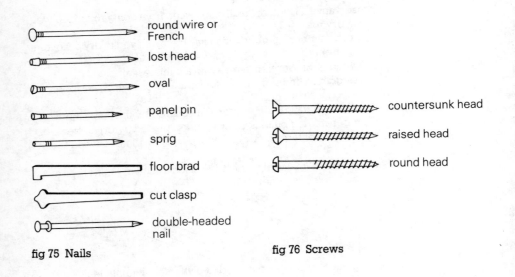

round wire or French

lost head

oval

panel pin

sprig

floor brad

cut clasp

double-headed nail

countersunk head

raised head

round head

fig 75 Nails   **fig 76 Screws**

5.5.c Tools

adjustable bevel (B7) see fig. 84
awl (B7) see fig. 85
bandsaw (B7) see fig. 83
bench (B5j) see fig. 77
bevelled edge chisel (B7) see fig. 78
bit (B7) see fig. 80
blade (B7) the part of a cutting tool which is sharpened for cutting
brace (B7) see fig. 80
chisel (B7) see fig. 78 for various types
combination square (B7) see fig. 84
compasses (B7) see fig. 84

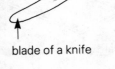

blade of a knife

cramp (B7) see fig. 79 for various types
drill (B7) tool for making holes; see fig. 80
electric chisel mortiser (B5j) machine for cutting wood joints
file (B7) see fig. 86
glasspaper (B7) sandpaper
gouge (B7) see fig. 78
hammer (B7) see fig. 81 for various types
lathe (B5j) see fig. 86
marking gauge (B7) see fig. 84
marking knife (B7) see fig. 84
mallet (B7) see fig. 81
nail punch (B7) see fig. 85
orbital sander (B7) electric sanding machine for cleaning wood
    surfaces or making them smooth; see fig. 86
pencil (B7) see fig. 84
pincers (B7) see fig. 85
plane (B7) see fig. 82 for various types
planing machine (B5j) machine for shaving the surface off wood to
    make it smooth
rasp (B7) see fig. 86
ratchet screwdriver (B7) see fig. 85
router (B5j) see fig. 82
sandpaper (B7) thick paper with a rough surface used for sanding
saw (B7) see fig. 83 for various types
scraper (B7) see fig. 86
screwdriver (B7) see fig. 85
sharpening stone (B7) see fig. 78
spokeshave (B7) see fig. 82
steel measuring tape or **steel rule** (B7) see fig. 85
tapered tang (B7) part of a tool which fits into a wooden handle
trammel (B7) see fig. 84
try square (B7) see fig. 84
twist bit (B7) see fig. 80
vice (B5j) see fig. 77
wooden rule (B7) see fig. 85

tang

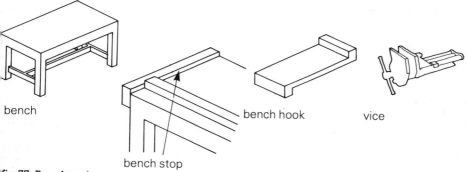

bench

bench hook   vice

bench stop

fig 77 Bench tools

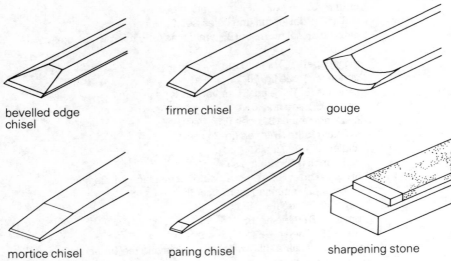

bevelled edge chisel

firmer chisel

gouge

mortice chisel

paring chisel

sharpening stone

fig 78 Chisels and gouges

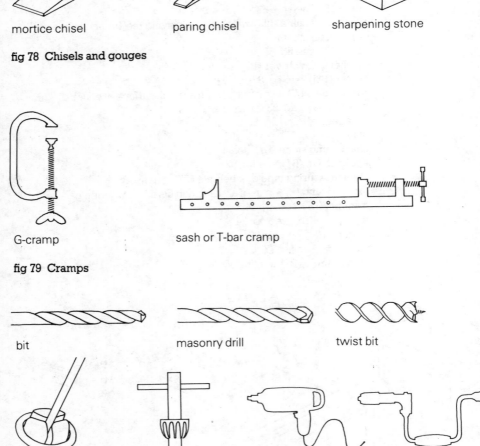

G-cramp

sash or T-bar cramp

fig 79 Cramps

bit

masonry drill

twist bit

jaws

chuck key

electric drill

brace

fig 80 Drills

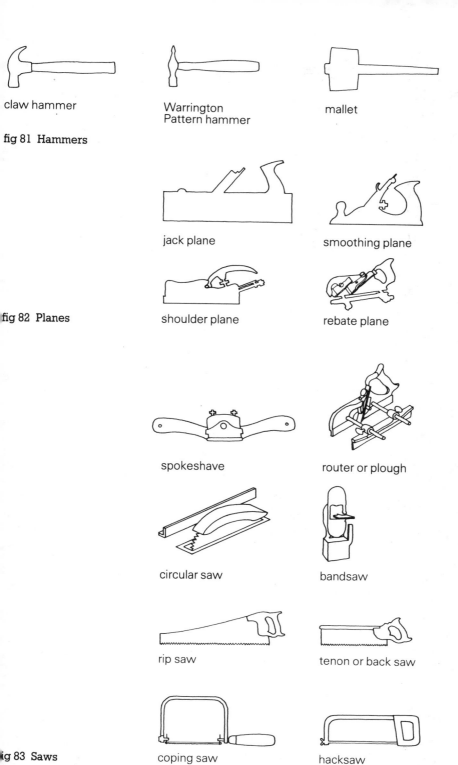

claw hammer

Warrington
Pattern hammer

mallet

fig 81 Hammers

jack plane

smoothing plane

fig 82 Planes

shoulder plane

rebate plane

spokeshave

router or plough

circular saw

bandsaw

rip saw

tenon or back saw

fig 83 Saws

coping saw

hacksaw

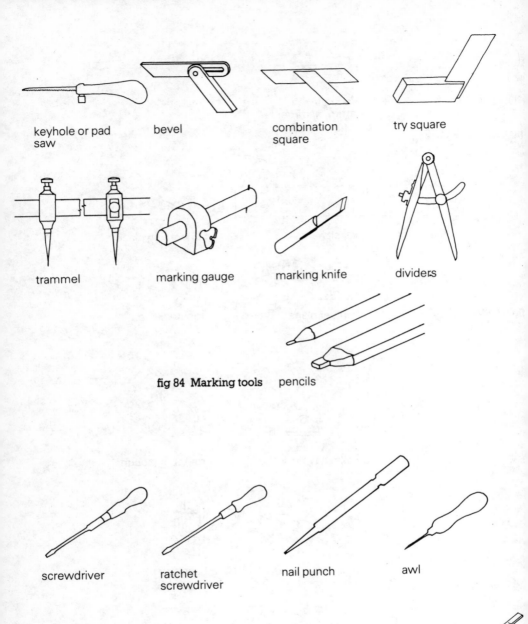

keyhole or pad saw

bevel

combination square

try square

trammel

marking gauge

marking knife

dividers

fig 84 Marking tools pencils

screwdriver

ratchet screwdriver

nail punch

awl

pincers

steel rule or tape

wooden rule

fig 85 Other hand tools

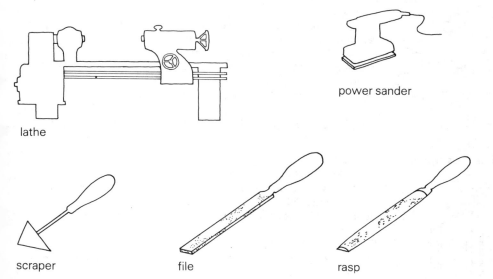

lathe

power sander

scraper

file

rasp

fig 86 Shaping and smoothing tools

5.5.d Actions

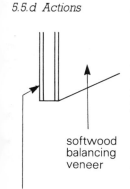

softwood
balancing
veneer

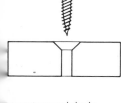

hardwood veneer

balancing a board Ri(d5) glueing a veneer to the back of a board to balance a finishing veneer on the front, so that the board will not bend

chiselling i(D4) cutting with a chisel

countersinking i(D4) shaping a screw hole to fit the head of the screw

drilling a hole i(D4) making a hole using a drill

hanging a door (32)(D6) fixing a door to its frame by hinges (butts)

letting in a screw t6(D6) fixing a screw with its head below the surface of the wood

kiln drying i(D2) reducing the moisture content of water in a heated space (kiln)

knotting v1(D6) painting a sealant over a knot in timber

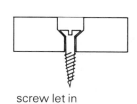

countersunk hole

screw let in

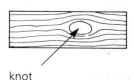

knot

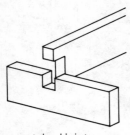

notched joint

notching i(D4) a simple way of making a wood joint
pelleting vl(D6) filling a hoe where a screw has been let in
planing i(D4) smoothing wood with a plane
plugging (D4) making a hole in a hard material for a screw fixing
sanding i(D4) smoothing wood with sandpaper
sawing i(D4) cutting wood with a saw
scribing timber i(D4) cutting timber to fit a surface which is not flat or straight, eg an uneven wall
selecting timber i(D2) choosing a piece of timber which is good enough for the job to be done
stopping timber vl(D6) filling knotholes or nail holes to match the timber

5.5.e Doors (32)

architrave (32.5) trim to cover the edge of the frame in a door or window; see fig. 88
door frame (32.5) frame to which a door is fixed by hinges
door furniture (32.9) ironmongery for a door, eg door handles
doorset (32.5) door and frame complete with ironmongery made up at a factory
fanlight (32.5) glazed panel above a door
fire-check door (32.5) door able to keep fire out for a certain period of time, eg half-hour fire door
flush door (32.5) see fig. 87
ledged and braced door (32.5) see fig. 87
muntin (32.5) see fig. 87
panelled door (32.5) see fig. 87
rebated door (32.5) door with a rebated edge
storey frame (32.5) door frame which is as high as the ceiling, usually with a fanlight at the top
weather bar (31.5) see fig. 88
weather board (31.5) see fig. 88

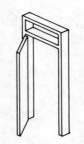

doorset
(storey frame)

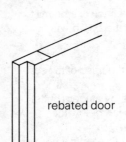

rebated door

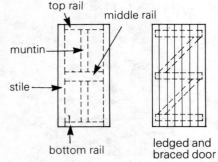

top rail

middle rail

muntin

stile

bottom rail

ledged and
braced door

flush door

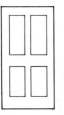

panelled door

fig 87 Door types

106

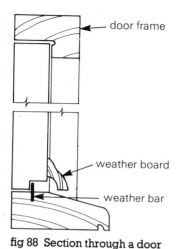

← door frame

← weather board

← weather bar

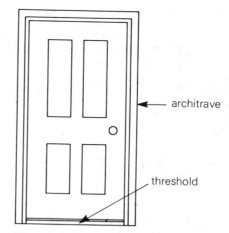

← architrave

threshold

fig 88 Section through a door   **Elevation of a door**

5.5.f Windows (31)   **bay window** (31.4) large window with three sides
bow window (31.4) curved window
casement window (31.4) window with opening lights which are
    hinged at the side or at the top
cill (31.4) bottom of a window; the cill allows water to drip off the
    window without running down the side of the building
double hung sash window (31.4) window with two sashes which slide
    up and down
drip channel (31.4) groove in the bottom of a window cill which
    makes water drip off
fixed light (31.4) part of a window which does not open
opening light (31.4) part of a window which opens
pivot window (31.4) window with an opening light hinged in the
    middle
pointing mastic t4 substance used to seal the gap between a window
    and the window opening
sash (31.4) an opening light which opens by sliding
side hung window (31.4) casement window with hinges at the side
sill (31.4) cill
top hung window (31.4) casement window with hinges at the top

bay window

bow window

casement
window

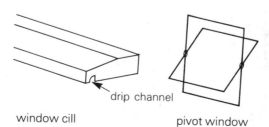

window cill

drip channel

pivot window

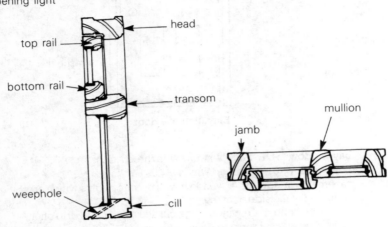

fixed light   transom

mullion

opening light

transom(e) (31.4) horizontal member in a window frame
weatherstrip (31.4) rubber or plastic strip to make an opening light airtight when closed
window frame (31.4) see fig. 89
weephole (31.4) small hole at the bottom of a window frame to allow water to drain to the cill

head

top rail

bottom rail

transom

mullion

jamb

weephole

cill

fig 89 Section through a window frame/frame

Plan of a window frame

5.5.g Stairs (24)

apron lining (34) see fig. 90
baluster (34) vertical handrail support
balustrade (34) handrail with balusters
flight of stairs (24) a number of steps all together
going (24) see fig. 90
handrail (34) hand hold at the side of a flight of stairs
newel (24) see fig. 90
nosing (24) see fig. 90
open riser (24) the space between two treads in an open tread staircase
rise (24) see fig. 90
staircase (24) flight of stairs

handrail

baluster

balustrade

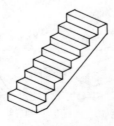

flight of stairs or staircase

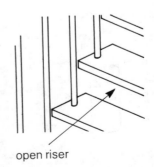

open riser

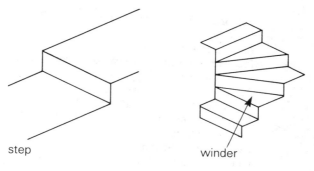

step   winder

step (24) tread with riser
string (24) the structural member at the side of a timber staircase
tread (24) see fig. 90
winder (24) step on a bend in a staircase

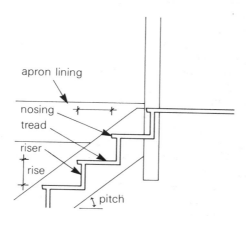

fig 90 Section through a staircase

5.5.h General

actual size the size of a piece of finished timber, ie after it has been planed
annual ring i line of wood grain, showing one year's growth of the tree
arris edge, eg 'arris to be lightly sanded'
battening Hi see fig. 91
carcassing Hi framing for a timber fitting, eg cupboard; vanitory shelf
centreing timber formwork for an arch
chamfer a sloping finish to an edge
counter battening Hi see fig. 91
cupboard storage cabinet
dry rot (merulius lacrymans) i fungus which destroys timber

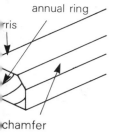

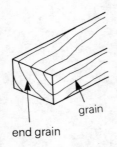

end grain

grain

end grain i the surface of a piece of wood which has been cut across the grain

finished size actual size

first fixing the first jobs a carpenter is able to finish in a building, eg door linings, timber grounds, carcassing

flame retardant not easily catching fire

formwork moulds for casting concrete

grain i lines and marks formed in timber as the tree grows

groove small channel

herringbone strutting Hi see fig. 92

joint Zi see timber joint

joist (29)Hi structural timber forming a floor or ceiling

joist hanger (23.9)h metal support for the end of a joist

knot i round mark in the grain of wood

lipping Hi bead fixed to the edge of a door or board to protect it; lipping is often hardwood

moulding Hi length of timber with a decorative shape

nogging Hi timber fixed between joists to which is fixed floor, ceiling, or roof board

nominal size size of a piece of timber before it has been planed

panelling Ri large boards used as a wall finish

planed timber i timber which has been made smooth with a plane

pressure impregnation u3 method of forcing timber preservative into the wood

pugging (23)C heavy material (eg sand) laid between timber floor joists for sound insulation

rabbet rebate

rebate edge of a piece of timber with part of the wood cut away

sawdust i particles of wood caused by sawing wood

sawn timber i timber with a rough finish, having been cut with a saw

seasoned timber i timber which has been allowed to dry out slowly

second fixing the jobs a carpenter does when a building is nearly finished, eg fixing skirting boards, hanging doors

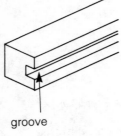

groove

joist hanger

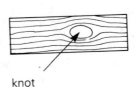

knot

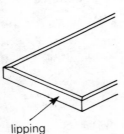

lipping

panelling

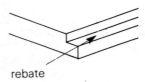

rebate

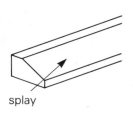

splay

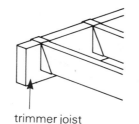

trimmer joist

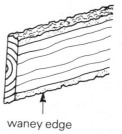

waney edge

skirting board Hi timber board which covers the joint between a floor finish and a wall finish

splay large chamfer

timber defect i see fig. 94 for various types

timber grounds i rough timber fixed to or built into a structure to which a fitting is screwed later on

timber joint Zi see fig. 93 for various types

trimmer joist (23)i strong joist which supports other joists fixed at a right angle (90°) to it

veneer i5 thin slice of good quality wood used on the face of a cheap board

waney edge i rough edge of a board with the bark of the tree on it

wet rot i fungus which destroys timber which has become wet

woodworm (Anobium Punctatum) small beetle which makes holes in timber

wood shaving i thin slice of wood removed by a plane

wrot timber i planed timber

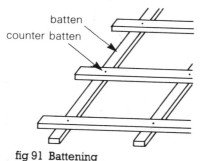

fig 91 Battening

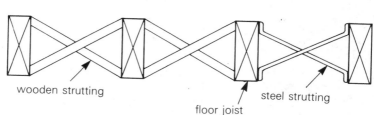

fig 92 Herringbone strutting

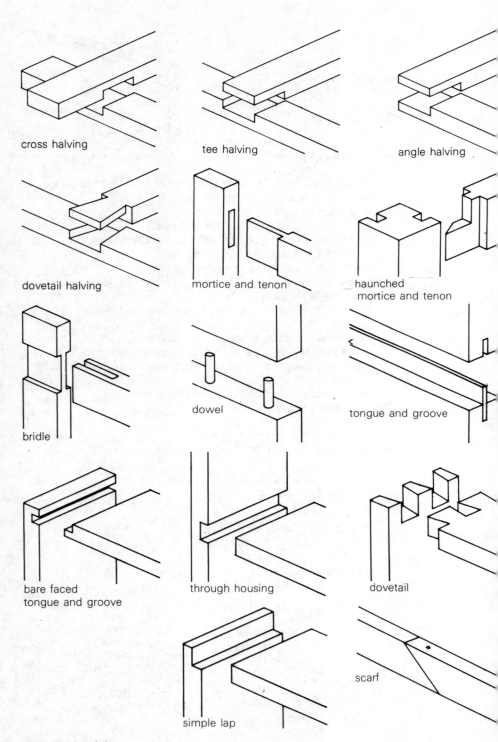

cross halving

tee halving

angle halving

dovetail halving

mortice and tenon

haunched
mortice and tenon

bridle

dowel

tongue and groove

bare faced
tongue and groove

through housing

dovetail

simple lap

scarf

fig 93 Timber joints

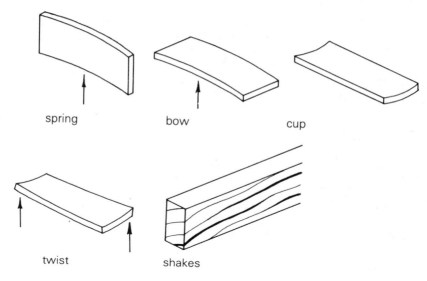

spring | bow | cup

twist | shakes

fig 94 Timber defects

5.6 *Ironmongery t7*

ball catch door catch suitable for a cupboard door

barrel bolt plain door bolt

butt device by which a door is fixed to its frame; usually sold as a pair of (2) butts

casement fastener fitting which holds a window shut

casement stay fitting which holds a window open

door closer fitting which allows a door to be opened, but shuts it afterwards

floor spring door closer hidden in the floor

flush bolt bolt fixed into the edge of a door at the top or bottom

flush ring type of door pull handle; flush means that it does not stick out from the surface of the door

fusible link a catch which breaks when it gets hot in a fire; often used to hold fire doors open

handle see fig. 95 for various types

hinge butt

hook see fig. 96 for various types

indicator bolt door bolt which shows whether or not the room (a toilet or bathroom) is being used

ball catch

barrel bolt

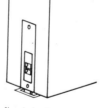

flush bolt

flush ring

kicking plate

knob

ironmongery t7 devices, usually metal, fixed to doors and windows
kicking plate metal plate fixed to the bottom of a door to protect it
    from heavy shoes
knob a door handle which must be held in the hand and turned
latch see fig. 97 for various types
letter plate hole in a door with a flap through which the postman
    delivers letters
lift-off butt hinge which enables the door to be lifted off without
    unscrewing the hinge
lock see fig. 98 for various types
numeral number
push plate metal plate fixed to the side of a door with which to push it
    open
rising butt hinge which acts as a door closer
selector fork fitting used on a pair of rebated doors with door closers
tee hinge large flat hinge

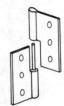

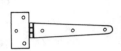

letter plate	lift-off butt	numeral	tee hinge

D-handle	grab handle	lever handle	knob handle

fig 95 Handles

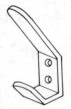

coat hook   hat and coat hook

fig 96 Hooks

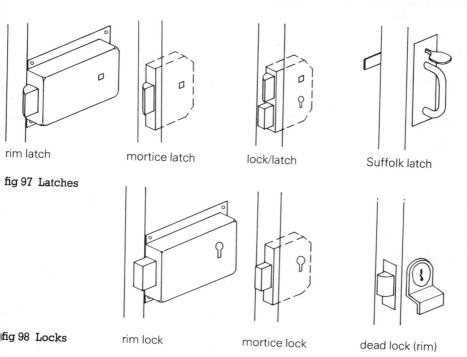

rim latch   mortice latch   lock/latch   Suffolk latch

fig 97 Latches

fig 98 Locks   rim lock   mortice lock   dead lock (rim)

5.7 Carpentry and Joinery

Drawings and Specifications

handing doors

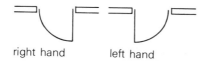

right hand   left hand

opening lights (windows)

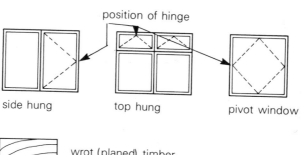

position of hinge

side hung   top hung   pivot window

ymbols

wrot (planed) timber

unwrot timber

6   Finishes

Language Practice

6.1.a Wall Finishes

'Mistakes in solid concrete are hard to put right'
When concrete work is not done correctly, a great deal of time and effort may be needed to remove the concrete and cast it again. The architect has to decide whether or not the mistake is serious enough to make this necessary.

fig 99

Peter – *Site Agent*   Norman – *Architect*
(Charlie – *Concrete Finisher*)

Peter There's no excuse for Charlie's mistake, I'm afraid. I'm very sorry about it. He finished the balcony wall, you see, and just went on bush-hammering round the corner and down the stair wall here without thinking.

Norman Well, it really is a stupid mistake. You'll have to put it right, you know, and that won't be easy. But you know that, don't you?

Peter Yes, I do realise. I was just wondering if there *was* anything we could do about it. There's no way of changing that finish, is there?

Norman Oh no, I'm afraid not. And we can't leave it as it is. It won't look right.

116

Peter Hmm. Yes, I suppose you're right. So it'll mean rebuilding the whole staircase then, will it?

Norman Well – that would be an awful lot more work for you, wouldn't it? No, it won't be necessary for you to do that, I don't think. Er – we can try bush-hammering everything else to match instead – you know, all the stair walls on all four staircases.

Peter Oh, that wouldn't be too bad, then. We'd better put Charlie on it, seeing as he did it wrong in the first place. I'll see he's more careful in future, anyway.

Norman Yes, you'd better keep an eye on him! Now, what else is there to look at?

Peter Well, the fair-faced and board-marked concrete walls have just had the shuttering removed. Perhaps you'd like to come and see them too.

board-marked concrete *see* 6.6.d	**fair-faced** *see* 6.6.d
bush-hammer *see* 6.6.c **bush-hammering**	**keep an eye on** watch closely
cast *see* 2.6.c **cast concrete**	**match** be the same
effort work, labour	**realise** understand
excuse good reason	**remove** take away
	shuttering *see* 2.6.d
	wonder think about

Answer the questions.

1 What careless mistake has Charlie made?
2 Why can't it be left as it is?
3 What does Peter think they will have to do to put the mistake right?
4 What does Norman suggest instead?
5 Who will do all the rest of the bush-hammering?
6 What else is ready for Norman to look at?

Peter is telling Sid what happened when Charlie did too much bush-hammering. Fill in the blanks.

I put Charlie on .... this morning. I'm afraid he made a bit of a mistake though, because he .... .I wondered .... , but Norman said it couldn't be changed. So I thought we'd have to .... , but Norman told us to .... instead. After that Norman and I went to ....

6.1.b '-ing' forms or infinitives after certain verbs

Look at these sentences from the conversation. The meaning of the phrase in *italics* is explained in brackets ( ) after each sentence.

A

He *went on bush-hammering* round the corner and down the stair wall. (He had been bush-hammering before he got to the corner, too)	*go on* + *-ing* = continue
It'll *mean rebuilding* the whole staircase (The whole staircase will have to be rebuilt)	*mean* + *-ing* = be a matter of
We can *try bush-hammering* everything else to match. (We'll see if that works)	*try* + *-ing* = experiment with

117

In these A sentences the verb is followed by an '-ing' form. Now look at the B sentences where the same verbs are followed by an infinitive instead, and the meaning is different.

B
> The men took down the shuttering and *went on to bush-hammer* the stair walls. (They hadn't been bush-hammering before)
>
> *go on to* = progress to
>
> I *mean to rebuild* the whole staircase. (That is my intention)
>
> *mean to* = intend to
>
> We'll *try to finish* this by the end of the day. (But we don't know if we will finish it)
>
> *try to* = attempt to

It is useful to know how to use these verbs correctly. Practise doing so in the following exercise.

Example:
Peter told Norman what Charlie had been doing and went on (explain) what had been done wrong.
Peter told Norman what Charlie had been doing, and went on to explain what had been done wrong.

---

1 When Charlie bush-hammered the stair wall by mistake, it meant (do) a lot more bush-hammering.

2 Norman tried (find) the best solution when Charlie did too much bush-hammering.

3 Charlie meant (work) carefully, but he forgot to look at the drawing.

4 Perhaps we should try (use) a different finish on the stair walls.

5 Charlie will go on (bush-hammer) the stair walls until he has finished all four.

6 The architect and the site agent finished looking at the bush-hammering and went on (look at) some other concrete walls.

6.2.a Floor Finishes

'You do it that way, I do it this way'
There are more ways than one of doing some jobs, and each tradesman chooses to use the method which he has found to be the quickest and the best.

fig 100

George – *Foreman Tiler*   Dave – *Tiler*

Dave I don't often use this semi-dry method to lay tiles. It seems to take me a long time. Do you always do it this way?

George Oh yes, I've usually found it works best. What do you think of it?

Dave Well, I can't say I'm very keen on it. Have you ever tried any other methods? On my last job we used a separating layer – you know, we laid the tiles on to polythene sheeting over a screed. It seemed to work really well.

George Hmm . . . yes, I've sometimes done it that way myself.

Dave We never got any cracking because of differential movement that way.

George Well, you don't my way either. Besides, with your method there are two parts to the job. First you've got to level your screed accurately, and then level your tiles accurately afterwards, haven't you? That all takes time.

Dave Well, your method has two stages too, if you think about it. You've got to make all your semi-dry mix first, and get it laid, and then you've got to start mixing your grout to bed the tiles on. And you've still got to fill and grout the joints afterwards with some of each mix.

George But listen, if you're laying screeds, you've always got to leave them to dry out, haven't you? It's a waste of time, that is, when you're working on a small area.

Dave I don't know about that.

George Well, if we compare the two methods next week, mine will be quicker ninety per cent of the time. You just see if I'm right.

Dave Okay, guvnor, you win – we'll stick to the semi-dry method.

---

bed *see* 6.5.c **bedding floor tiles**

cracking breaking along a line

differential movement *see* 6.5.d

grout *see* 6.5.a

guvnor (Governor) boss, chief

keen on fond of, happy about

level make flat

polythene sheeting *see* 6.5.a

screed *see* 6.5.d

semi-dry method *see* 6.5.d

separating layer *see* 6.5.d

stage one part of a process

stick to continue using

tile *see* 6.5.a

Answer the questions.

1 What method does George always use to lay tiles? Why does he prefer this method?

2 What method does Dave usually use?

3 What can cause cracking with some methods of laying tiles?

4 What are the two stages of laying tiles Dave's way?

5 What are the two mixes used in George's method?

6 Why does George think it is a waste of time to use Dave's method on a small area?

Complete the sentences.

1 Dave doesn't usually use the semi-dry method to lay tiles because
....

2 On his last job the method he used was ....

3 Dave thinks it is a good method because ....

4 George thinks Dave's method takes longer because ....
....

5 If Dave's method is going to work properly, then........................
.... , which wastes time.

6 George is sure that his method is quicker most of the time, so
....

6.2.b Position of adverbs of frequency

Look at these sentences:

A My method isn't *always* quicker.

B We *always* use this method.

C We shan't *always* be using this method.

D I *always* used to use a different method.

With adverbs of frequency (always, sometimes, never ever, usually, often, etc) there are special problems about word order. There is no simple rule to tell us where they should go in the sentence. From the four sentences above we can make these four rules:

1 They come *after* simple tenses of 'to be' (A)

2 They come *before* simple tenses of all other verbs (B)

3 They come *after* the *first* part of any verb with more than one part (C)

4 They usually come before 'used to' and 'have to' (D)

Look through the conversation again. Can you find examples of adverbs of frequency in use? Now try to put the adverbs of frequency in the right place in these sentences:

Example:

I used to find the semi-dry method best. (often)

I often used to find the semi-dry method best.

1 Do you get differential movement with this method? (ever)

2 You have to level the screed accurately when using a separating layer. (always)

3 It is a waste of time to leave screeds to dry out. (usually)

4 With the semi-dry method you've got to grout the joints at the end. (always)

5 I used direct tiling on my last jobs. (sometimes)

6 It was quicker using the semi-dry method. (always)

6.3.a Ceiling Finishes

'Accuracy is the finishing tradesman's chief skill'

Most work on a building site does not require perfect accuracy. When an error is made, the decision to rectify it often depends upon whether the mistake will be noticed.

Sid – *Clerk of Works*   Bernard – *Ceiling Fixer*   (Tim – *Apprentice Ceiling Fixer*)   (Peter – *Site Agent*)

Sid I say, Bernard, I don't like the look of this at all. You haven't got

fig 101

the ceiling grid very level, you know. You'll have to do something about it, or I'll be reporting it to Peter.

Bernard Oh, I'm sorry, Sid – I'm afraid I hadn't noticed it was out. I didn't fix this bit, you see. Tim did most of it and I haven't got around to checking it with the spirit level yet.

Sid You can see it's out quite clearly from up here on the step ladder. You'd better have a look yourself.

Bernard Hmm, yes, it doesn't look quite right, I'll give you that.

Sid Will it be a lot of work to put it right?

Bernard Well, that depends really. The suspension hangers are adjustable, but obviously we have to take off the panels and hold-down clips to get at them. It just depends how many need adjusting – it could take ages.

Sid Oh dear.

Bernard Couldn't we just leave it as it is, Sid? I don't think anyone'll notice. It looks almost level to me.

Sid Oh no, definitely not. It just won't do, I'm afraid. There are going to be wall lights in here, so any sagging in the ceiling will really show up.

Bernard Oh well, I suppose we'd better get on with it right away.

Sid Yes. And don't forget the electricians are waiting to start on this ceiling as soon as you've finished.

ceiling grid *see* 6.7.c
depend vary according to circumstances
electrician *see* 0.1
error mistake
get around to find time to
get at reach, have access to
get on with make a start on
hold-down clip *see* 6.7.a
I'll give you that I agree
notice see, catch sight of
out not accurate

rectify put right
report give information about
sagging sinking down in the middle
show up be easily seen
spirit level *see* 2.5.c
step ladder *see* 8.5.b
suspension hanger *see* 6.7.a

Answer the questions.

1 Why is Sid not satisfied with the ceiling?
2 Who did most of the work on the ceiling?
3 Why hasn't Bernard noticed the mistake?
4 Where is Sid standing?
5 How do they get at the suspension hangers?
6 Why can't they leave it as it is?

Write Bernard's part of the conversation.

Sid Have you checked over this ceiling yet?

Bernard ....

Sid No, it isn't. Here, get up on this step ladder and have a look for yourself.

Bernard ....

Sid Well, it doesn't matter who did it, does it? It'll have to be put right all the same. Is it a long job adjusting those suspension hangers?

Bernard ....

Sid I see . . . so it could take a long time.

Bernard ....

Sid Of course it'll have to be done. There are going to be wall lights in here, you know.

Bernard ....

Sid They're waiting to start as soon as you've finished, so you'd better get on with it.

6.3.b Using 'get'

In spoken English 'get' is used in a number of different ways. Look at these sentences from the conversation:

I haven't *got around to* checking it with the spirit level yet. (*Get around to*: find time to)

We have to take off the panels . . . to *get at* them.
(*Get at*: reach, have access to)

I suppose we'd better *get on with* it right away.
(*Get on with*: make a start on, or continue with, sometimes in a hurry)

We use phrases with 'get' all the time in conversation. Practise the ones above in this exercise. Choose the correct phrase to complete the sentence.

Example:

Bernard I'm afraid I've been a bit busy this morning. I haven't ....
.... checking this ceiling is level yet.

Bernard *I'm afraid I've been a bit busy this morning. I haven't got around to checking this ceiling is level yet.*

1 **Sid** Will you have to take all those panels off to ....
.... the suspension hangers?
2 **Bernard** One of these days I'll .... showing Tim how to level a ceiling properly.
3 **Bernard** After we've done this ceiling in the dining room we'll have to .... the ones in the offices.
4 **Bernard** Peter hasn't .... coming down to inspect this ceiling yet.

5 **Sid** You'll have to .... straightening out the
ceiling as quickly as you can. You know the electrician is
waiting to start in here too.

6 **Sid** Leave the panels out when you've finished so the electrician
can .... his wiring.

Communication on Site

6.4.a Pointing out mistakes

Finding fault, admitting and denying and putting right

Sometimes on site, work is not done according to the specification, or
mistakes are made. Sometimes we have to point out someone else's
mistake. Here are some ways we might do it:

This won't do, you know.
I don't like the look of this at all.
I'm sorry, but you'll have to put it right, you know.
This isn't good enough, I'm afraid.
It just isn't up to scratch/up to standard.
It's not satisfactory. We can't leave it like this.
You'll have to do something about this.

When mistakes are pointed out to us, we might agree like this:

Oh yes, I see what you mean.
Yes, I think you're right.
Now you come to mention it . . .
You could be right there.
I'm afraid I hadn't noticed that.

Or, if we already know about it, we might say:

Oh yes, I know about that already.
Yes, I've just spotted it myself.
Yes, I know. We'll be seeing to it later.
Yes, I was just wondering what we could do about it.

Look through conversations 6.1.a and 6.3.a to see where some of these
expressions are used. Now look at Sid and Bernard talking about the
ceiling grid:

Sid Hey, Bernard, you'll have to do something about this ceiling. It
just doesn't look right, you know.

Bernard Hmm . . . now you come to mention it, it doesn't seem quite
level, does it?

Write short conversations on this pattern for all the following
situations. Try to practise using as many different expressions as you
can.

1 The stair wall has been bush-hammered by mistake.
Dennis Charlie! What have you been doing? . . . . .

2 The wall tiles have been put up and the pattern isn't quite right.
George Now, Dave, I told you to check before you started putting
these up . . . . .

3 There are air-bubbles in the surface of one of the concrete walls.
Peter Well, I'm sorry, Charlie, but . . . . .

4 Some of the joints between the tiles have not been grouted.
George Look here, Dave . . . . .

123

5 Sid is showing Jimmy, the plasterer, where one of the walls has been badly finished.

    Sid Just look at this wall, Jimmy . . . . .

6 Some vinyl floor tiles have come a bit unstuck.

    George I'm afraid these tiles don't look very good, Dave . . . . .

6.4.b Excuses and apologies

If we are responsible for a mistake, we may admit it with an excuse or explanation, and often an apology, like this:

I'm sorry, I'm afraid it was done before I realised.

I'm sorry, I didn't realise it had to be done like that.

I'm very sorry. I'm afraid I wasn't thinking what I was doing.

I hadn't realised it was wrong, I'm afraid.

I *am* sorry. I'm afraid I wasn't here when it was done this morning.

Or, if we feel the mistake is not our responsibility, we might deny it and say instead:

Well, it wasn't me working on that bit, you know.

I'm sorry, but it's not my fault.

I'm afraid I don't know anything about it.

It's nothing to do with me – you'd better see Peter about it.

Well, I'm sure *I* didn't leave it like that.

Using the same six situations as before, write short conversations to practise admitting and denying. You can use the same opening speeches as you used the first time, and make up two replies for each one.

Example:

Sid Hey, Bernard, you'll have to do something about this ceiling. It just doesn't look right, you know.

Bernard (*Admitting*) I'm sorry, I hadn't realised it was wrong, I'm afraid.

    (*Denying*) Well, I didn't fix this bit, you know. It's not my fault.

6.4.c. Putting things right

When work is not done correctly, suggestions are made or instructions given to put things right. Here are some things we might say:

I think you'd better . . . . .

Well, I'd like you to . . . . .

It'll mean . . . . . , you know.

We can always try . . . . .

Why don't you . . . . . ?

Perhaps the solution would be . . . .

You'll have to . . . . .

For more detail on making suggestions and giving instructions, see 1.4 and 2.4.

Look at this conversation between Sid and Bernard:

Sid Hey, Bernard, you'll have to do something about this ceiling. It just doesn't look right, you know.

Bernard Oh, doesn't it? I'm sorry, I'm afraid I haven't had time to check it yet.

Sid Well, you'd better try adjusting the suspension hangers to see if you can get it level.

Use the same situations as before and write conversations on this pattern to practise suggestions and instructions. Use your own ideas for putting the problem right.

6.5 Floor Finishes
(43)

6.5.a Materials and Components

roll of broadloom carpet

carpet tile

broadloom carpet (43)T carpet in wide lengths
carpet (43)T soft floor covering
carpet tile (43)T small piece of carpet
ceramics g2 products made from fired clay
ceramic floor tile (43)Sg2 clay floor tile, often with a glazed (glass) finish
cork j5 natural material which is the bark of a tree; cork is used to make floor and wall tiles
grout type of cement used to fill the joints in floor tiling
latex n5 rubber
linoleum (lino) (43)Tn4 sheet floor covering on a hessian backing
mastic asphalt (43)s4 waterproof material for roofing and flooring; asphalt forms a hard floor suitable for industrial buildings
matwell recess in floor in which a doormat may be laid
quarry tile (43)Sg2 plain clay floor tile
rubber flooring (43)Tn5 flooring sheets or tiles made from rubber or synthetic rubber, often with a studded finish
tile (43)S piece of flat material used as floor or wall finish
tongue and groove (t. & g.) board Hi2 timber board used as floor boards, or as a wall or ceiling finish
underlay (43)T soft sheet material laid below a carpet
vinyl n6 hard plastic used to make floor tiles

matwell frame

studs

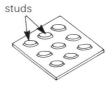

rubber floor tile

tongue and groove board

6.5.b Tools

nail punch

concrete edging trowel (B7) see fig. 102
finishing sander (B7) see fig. 102
flooring trowel (B7) see fig. 102
nail punch (B7) hand tool used for secret nailing
power float (B6) machine used on concrete after pouring to form a smooth, flat surface; see fig. 102
screeding batten (B7) straight piece of wood to form a smooth surface on a screed

6.5.c Actions

bedding floor tiles (D6) placing floor tiles in position
direct bedding (D6) laying floor tiles on a thin layer of adhesive
floor laying (D6) putting in place any floor finish
grouting floor tiles (D6) filling the joints in floor tiles with tile grout
laying a floor finish (D6) floor laying

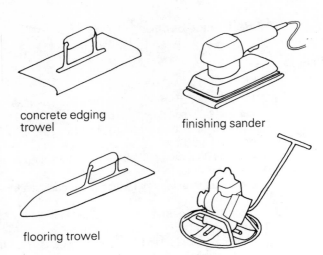

concrete edging
trowel

finishing sander

flooring trowel

power float

fig 102 Floor finishing tools

screeding (D6) laying a screed
secret nailing (D6) fixing timber boards so that the nails cannot be
seen; see fig. 103

6.5.d General

bay area of tiling or screeding laid at one time
differential movement movement of different materials at different
rates, caused by heat or moisture

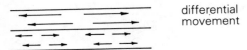

differential
movement

going off cement and concrete 'goes off' when it first begins to
harden
granolithic (43)q5 hard concrete floor finish containing chips of
granite (a type of stone)
hardwood strip flooring (43)i3 see fig. 103
latex screed (43)q2 sand/cement screed containing latex (rubber) to
form a thin, strong screed
parquet flooring (43)i3 wood block flooring
penny gap Z small gap between two timber boards, which allows
expansion (movement); see fig. 103
screed (43) smooth, flat finish to a concrete floor, usually made of
sand and cement; see fig. 104
semi-dry method way of laying clay floor tiles; see fig. 104
separating layer (43) sheet of plastic used in laying clay floor tiles;
see fig. 104
terrazzo (43)q5 concrete floor finish containing chips of marble (a
type of stone)
wood block flooring (43)i3 floor finish of pieces of hardwood

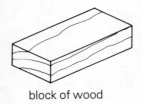

block of wood

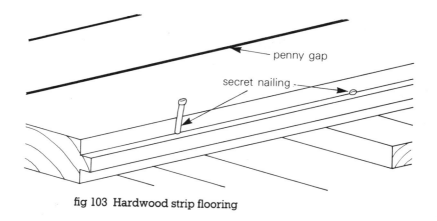

fig 103 Hardwood strip flooring

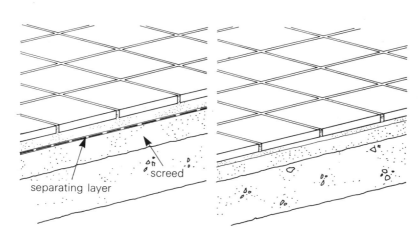

fig 104 Clay tiling

6.6 Wall Finishes
(42)

6.6.a Materials and Components

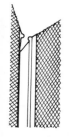

corner plaster
bead

roll of hessian

cement q2 binding material used to make concrete, and used in some plaster mixes

ceramic wall tile (42)g2 clay wall tile, often with a glazed (glass) finish

coarse stuff plasterer's name for materials like sand and lime

corner plaster bead Jh expanded metal strip used to form a neat corner in plastering

expanded metal lath Jh steel mesh used to put plaster on

hessian Tj3 coarse fabric used like wallpaper

can or tin of paint

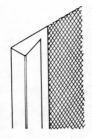

plaster stop bead

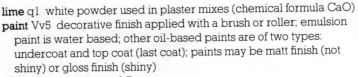

lime q1 white powder used in plaster mixes (chemical formula CaO)

paint Vv5 decorative finish applied with a brush or roller; emulsion paint is water based; other oil-based paints are of two types: undercoat and top coat (last coat); paints may be matt finish (not shiny) or gloss finish (shiny)

plasterboard Rr2 see 6.7.a

plaster Pr2 1. wet mix to form a smooth, hard wall finish

2. powder which forms a wet mix as above when mixed with water

plaster stop bead Jh metal plaster strip

primer Vv1 special paint to be the first coat used on wood or metal

sand p1 tiny rock particles, used in some plaster mixes

scrim T hessian or paper tape used to strengthen plaster, eg over a joint between sheets of plasterboard

sealer Vv1 primer paint used on materials which absorb (take in) a lot of paint, such as wood

tile adhesive t3 product used to fix ceramic tiles to a wall

tile cement t3 tile adhesive, usually a powder mixed with water

tongue and groove (t. & g.) board Hi2 timber board, usually vee-jointed for use as a wall finish

wallpaper (42)T wall finish made of paper or vinyl (plastic)

white spirit liquid added to oil paint to make it thinner

wood stain Vv2 coloured liquid wood finish which protects the wood from the weather

roll of scrim

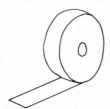

can or tin of tile adhesive

t. & g. board

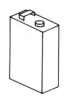

can or tin of wood stain

6.6.b Tools

paint brush

brush (B7) tool for applying paint

darby (B7) long tool for levelling plaster; see fig. 105

drag (B7) see fig. 105

gauging box (B4) container for measuring plaster mixes; see fig. 105

hand float (B7) see fig. 105

joint rule (B7) see fig. 105

lath hammer (B7) see fig. 105

pick hammer (B7) see fig. 105

roller (B7) tool for applying paint

scissors (B7) cutting tool

skimming float (B7) see fig. 105

spray (B5h) tool for applying paint

tile cutter (B7) tool for cutting wall tiles

trowel (B7) see fig. 106 for various types

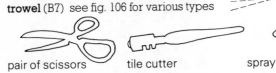

roller

pair of scissors   tile cutter   spray

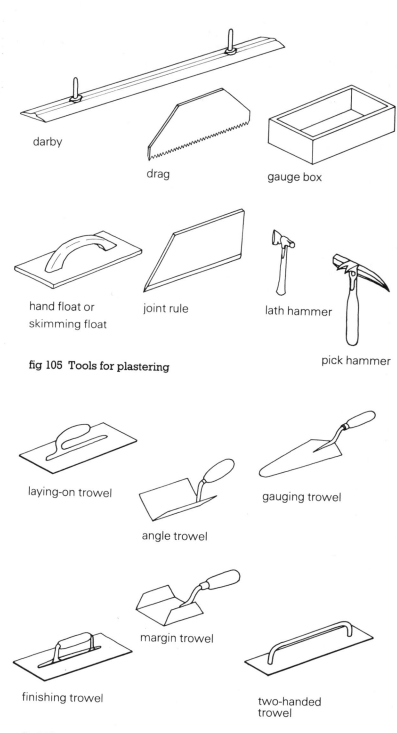

darby

drag

gauge box

hand float or
skimming float

joint rule

lath hammer

pick hammer

fig 105 Tools for plastering

laying-on trowel

angle trowel

gauging trowel

finishing trowel

margin trowel

two-handed
trowel

fig 106 Trowels

6.6.c Actions

tooled hammer
head

'point'

spray

applying paint or **plaster** (D6) putting paint or plaster on to a surface
bush-hammering (D5) tooling concrete with a toothed hammer head
dry lining (D6) fixing plasterboard sheets to brick or block walls as a
    wall finish
paperhanging (D6) glueing wallpaper to a wall
point tooling (D5) tooling concrete with a 'point'
projection plastering (D6) applying plaster to a surface using a spray
    machine
raking out (D6) cutting out joints in brickwork to give a good key for
    plastering
rendering (D6) applying a coat of cement/sand
retempering plaster (D4) adding water to a plaster mix which has
    become a little dry
ruling plaster (D6) using a straight length of wood to make a flat
    surface on plaster
scratching plaster (D6) making a rough surface on plaster as a key
    for the next coat
stippling plaster (D6) forming a plaster surface into small bumps
stirring paint (D4) turning paint in the can with a stick before using it
thinning paint (D4) adding liquid to paint which has become too thick
tooling concrete (D5) removing the surface from concrete with a
    mechanical hammer
trowelling plaster (D6) making a surface on plaster using a trowel

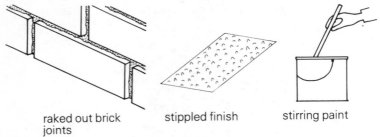

raked out brick
joints

stippled finish

stirring paint

6.6.d General

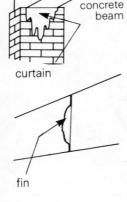

concrete
beam

curtain

fin

bleeding through Vv showing a paint on another coat of paint which
    has been applied on top
blow hole Eq4 air hole formed on the surface of concrete
board-marked concrete (42)Eq4 see fig. 107
coat layer of paint or plaster applied at one time
curtain Eq4 name for concrete which has run out of formwork down a
    wall
fair-faced F carefully finished block, brick, or concrete wall
fin Eq4 concrete which has run out of formwork at a joint in the
    formwork
finishing coat Vv the last coat of plaster to be applied to a surface
floating coat Pr2 the second (2nd) coat in 3-coat plaster work
initial set Pr hardening of plaster soon after it has been applied
key roughness of a surface so that plaster will stick to it
lath background surface on which plaster is applied
moulding Pr plaster formed to a shape
pencil rounded arris curved edge (small radius curve)

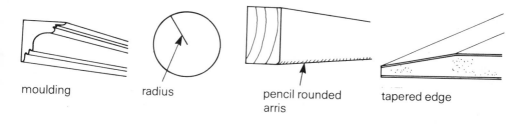

moulding   radius   pencil rounded   tapered edge
                        arris

ribbed concrete(42)Eq4 see fig. 107
shrinkage crack small crack formed in plaster after setting
skim coat Pr2 finishing coat of plaster
suction property of plaster to stick to a background surface, eg
    concrete has low suction, so a good key is needed
tapered edge edge of a sheet of plasterboard for dry lining
timber panelling Ri see 5.5.h **panelling**
tooled concrete Eq4 see 6.6.c **tooling concrete**
undercoat Vv see 6.6.a **paint**

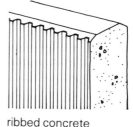

board-marked concrete   ribbed concrete

fig 107 Concrete finishes

6.7 Ceiling Finishes (45)

6.7.a Materials and Components

clout nail

ceiling panel (35.9) board fixed to a grid to form a suspended ceiling
clout nail t6 nail used to fix sheets of plasterboard to a ceiling or wall
edge trim (35.9) plastic or metal strip at the edge of a suspended
    ceiling
grid member (35.9) part of a suspended ceiling grid
hold down clip (35.9) clip to hold a ceiling panel in place
nailing plate (35.9) metal plate to fix a suspended ceiling grid to a
    timber joist

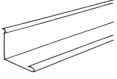

edge trim

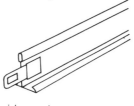

grid member

hold down clip

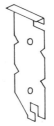

nailing plate

support clamp

plaster Pr2 see 6.6.a
plasterboard Rr2 rigid sheet made from gypsum between sheets of stiff paper; gypsum is a white, powdery substance
support clamp (35.9) metal bracket to hold an electric light fitting within a suspended ceiling
suspension hanger (35.9) metal part which fixes a suspended ceiling to the roof structure

6.7.b Actions

assembling a grid (D6) fixing a framework to support suspended ceiling panels
breaking joint (D6) fixing boards so that the joints are not in a line
square cutting (D4) cutting sheets to the right length or width

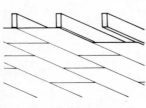

breaking joint

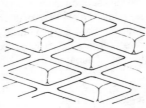

coffered ceiling

coving

6.7.c General

ceiling grid (35) framework to support ceiling panels
coffered ceiling ceiling with large recesses, eg ceiling formed by a waffle slab; see fig. 34
coving (45) trim at the edge of a ceiling
false ceiling (35) suspended ceiling
margin edge
suspended ceiling (35) ceiling hung from a structural floor, to leave a space above it
textured ceiling finish (45) material like thick paint which forms a hard, stippled or patterned ceiling finish

6.8 Finishes (43)

Drawings and Specifications

Finishes schedule (or **Finishing schedule**) chart or list of finishes to be applied to walls, floors and ceilings in each room of a building
internal elevation elevation showing the inside of a building
reflected ceiling plan plan of a ceiling drawn on a floor plan

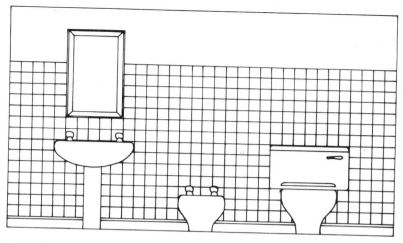

internal elevation of a bathroom

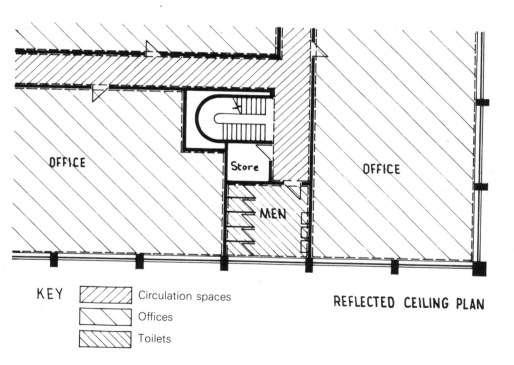

KEY

 Circulation spaces

Offices

Toilets

OFFICE

Store

MEN

OFFICE

REFLECTED CEILING PLAN

fig 108 Reflected ceiling plan

7 Plumbing and Drainage

Language Practice

7.1.a Drainage

'Check and double-check'
If a drain leaks after it has been covered up, a lot of work is needed to repair it again. It is better to test it properly first.

fig 109

Phil – *Foreman Drainlayer*   Alec – *Drainlayer*   (Sid – *Clerk of Works*)

Phil Are all these runs working all right, Alec?

Alec Well, Sid's just been over to check on this one between manhole 6 and manhole 7. We did an air test on it. Er – I'm afraid it's leaking a bit.

Phil Oh? What did Sid say about that, then?

Alec Well, it looked quite reasonable to me, actually, but he said it wasn't good enough. He thought the reading had gone down a bit too much. Sid always wants things just right, he does. So he said we'd have to trace the leak. He's coming to check again this afternoon.

Phil Hmm – that might take a time. Just look at the length of that run.

Alec Well – it's not too bad, really. Sid said to divide the run in the middle and test the two halves separately.

Phil Yes, that usually makes it quicker of course.

Alec You know, that's one big advantage of these sleeve joints over the old type. It's much easier to dismantle them to find a leak, isn't it?

Phil Yes. And the air test seems better than the old water test, I think. Much quicker as well.

Alec Oh yes, it is.

Phil And you can often hear something when there's a leak, can't you? That always helps when you don't know where to start looking.

air test *see* 7.5.c **testing drains**	**reasonable** all right, acceptable
advantage good point	**repair** mend
dismantle take apart	**run** length (of pipe)
divide split in two	**sleeve** *see* 7.5.a
leak allow water to pass through where it shouldn't	**trace** look for, find
	water test *see* 7.5.c **testing**
manhole *see* 7.5.d	**drains**
reading measurement recorded	

Answer the questions.

1 Why should drains be tested thoroughly?

2 What was the result of the air test on the run between manhole 6 and manhole 7?

3 Why did Sid think the leak would have to be traced?

4 How did Sid suggest tracing the leak?

5 What is the advantage of sleeve joints over the old type?

6 Why is the air test better than the old water test?

Fill in Sid's part of the conversation he had with Alec on site.

Alec Hello Sid. What can I do for you?

Sid ....

Alec Right. Well, we've done that air test now. Would you like to check the reading?

Sid ....

Alec It doesn't look too bad to me.

Sid ....

Alec That could take ages – look how long that run is.

Sid ....

Alec Well, that should make it quicker anyway.

Sid ....

Alec Yes, you're right – the old type were much harder to dismantle.

Sid ....

Alec Yes, I do. It seems so much quicker.

7.1.b Using present tenses

Look at these sentences from the conversation:

A   Sid always *wants* things just right.
   That usually *makes* it quicker, of course.

B   *Are* all these runs *working* all right?
   I'm afraid it's *leaking* a bit.

C   He's *coming* to check again this afternoon.

The A sentences use the *simple present* tense. This shows here habit or method, and may often be used with a frequency expression (always, often, never, etc). Questions in the simple present are formed with 'do'.

The B sentences use the *present continuous* which is formed with the verb 'to be' and an '-ing' form (You *are checking*, I *am looking*, *are* we *starting?* etc). This is used for an action going on at the present moment (now).

The C sentence shows how the *present continuous* can also be used for planned actions in the immediate future.

Can you find more examples of these tenses in the conversation? Practise using the different tenses correctly in this exercise.

Example:
Sid always (say) things have to be just right.
Sid always says things have to be just right.

1 Sid (come) to check on this run later.
2 Drains sometimes (leak) when they are first tested.
3 Alec (dismantle) the joint so he can find where the leak is.
4 The men usually (listen) for the sound of air escaping when they (test) the runs.
5 I don't think this drain run (work) properly.
6 I (try) to find the leak between manhole 6 and manhole 7.

7.2.a Cold Water Plumbing

'Pipes take up space'
It is not usually possible to show every component in a building on one drawing. As a result components may be shown on different drawings occupying the same space.

fig 110

Keith – *Foreman Plumber* Bert – *Plumber*

Bert Keith, there'll have to be some changes in this kitchen area. There's not really enough room to put in all the services the way they've been shown.

Keith Hmm – I can't say I'm surprised. We've got so many services here, what with the gas cookers and washing-up machines.

Bert That's just it. You see, the electrician's been in this morning. He's just shown me where he's marked his conduits out on the floor – you know, the ones supplying the room below. He was wondering if there was going to be enough room for my pipes too.

Keith Yes, you'll have to cross those conduits in a few places, won't you? Well, let's see, the screed will be 65 millimetres thick in here, so you can do it with pipes up to 22 millimetres in size.

Bert But they've got to be wrapped in lagging, remember. And in two places I need to cross a conduit with a 35 millimetre cold feed pipe. There's just not enough space.

Keith Then your pipes will have to be re-routed, and that conduit too, if necessary. I think you'd better get it all worked out on paper as soon as possible, and let me know what you come up with.

Bert Well actually, I've done it already, and marked it in on the drawing.

Keith Fine. If you hang on a minute, then, I'll get the resident engineer over here to approve it.

approve officially accept
cold feed pipe pipe which takes cold water into a tank or appliance, eg a washing machine
come up with work out
component part
conduit see fig. 135
electrician see 0.1
hang on a minute wait a minute
lagging see 7.6.e

mark draw, indicate
occupy take up
pipe see 7.6.b
re-route take on a different course
resident engineer see 0.1
screed see 6.5.d
service gas, electricity, water, drains, etc, in a building
wrap cover

Answer the questions.

1 Why does Bert think there will have to be changes in the kitchen area?
2 What services have to be brought to the kitchen?
3 What has the electrician been doing?
4 Why can't the pipes be laid the way they are shown?
5 What will be covering the pipes? What is this for?
6 Why does the resident engineer have to be brought over?

Fill in the blanks.

There are too many services coming to the kitchen area, so ....
.... The electrician isn't sure whether ....
.... The pipes are thicker than usual because ....
.... , and in two places ....
The foreman plumber says .... When a new
layout has been worked out, ...

.2.b Contracted erb forms

You know already that in spoken English we usually use a shortened (or contracted) form of certain verbs. Look at this sentence from the conversation:

There's not really enough room to put in all the services the way *they've* been shown.

It would sound unnatural if Bert were to say instead:

There is not really enough room to put in all the services the way *they have* been shown.

Look through the conversation and see where else contracted forms have been used (Can you work out what all these would be in full?)
Remember we don't use contracted verb forms:

1 if the verb is stressed:

I'll finish this tomorrow (unstressed)
I *will* finish this tomorrow! (stressed 'will')

2 if the verb is a question:

He's a plumber (statement)
Is he a plumber? (question)

Remember also that 'not' can be shortened to 'n't' and combined with many verbs (can't, doesn't, needn't, mustn't, hasn't, etc). Contractions with 'n't' can be questions as well as statements.

Practise using contractions in the answers you make up to these questions.

Example:
Has the electrician finished marking out his conduits yet? (not quite)
No, he hasn't quite finished them.

---

1 Will the electrician be coming today? (this afternoon)
2 Will all these pipes have to be lagged? (before the other services are put in)
3 Is this screed thick enough to take all the services? (not where two pipes have to cross)
4 Have you put in many services in the kitchen area? (all except the last of the pipework)
5 Are these conduits crossed by any cold feed pipes? (not in this building)
6 Will you work out how these services should be re-routed? (as soon as I can)

7.3.a Hot Water Plumbing

'Running hot and cold'

When a contractor completes a building, his work is not finished until it has been occupied for several months. This period is called the Defects Liability Period, and during this time some big mistakes can be discovered.

Norman – *Architect*   Peter – *Site Agent*   (Sid – *Clerk of Works*)

(Telephone conversation)

Norman Oh, hello, Peter. It's Norman here. I've just been down to the Cavendish Hotel Site. Er – Sid's been telling me all the latest problems with the plumbing.

Peter Oh, you mean the leaking shower wastes. Well, that was the manufacturer's fault, you know, and . . .

Norman No, actually, Sid says the shower wastes have already been seen to, no more problems there. In fact, he says the hotel itself seems fine now. It's the Manager's flat this time – he's just moved in.

Peter Oh yes? What's the trouble, then?

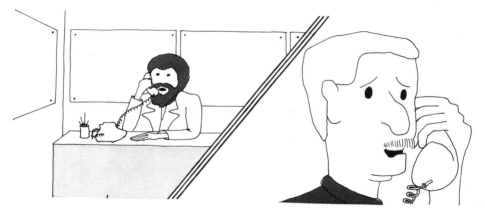

fig 111

Norman Oh, Peter, would you just hang on a minute? I'm afraid the other phone's ringing.
A moment later . . .
Norman Sorry about that. Now where was I?
Peter You were just telling me about the Manager's flat at the Cavendish.
Norman Ah yes. Well, you're not going to believe this, but the Manager said there was no hot water from the bath or basin.
Peter What?
Norman Well, that's not quite true, actually. We ran all the taps just now, and the *cold* tap on the bath ran hot.
Peter Oh no! What a stupid mistake. Well, fortunately it'll only be a question of changing over the tap heads. I can send someone down to fix that straight away.
Norman Ah yes, but you haven't heard it all yet. The basin has no hot at all.
Peter I don't believe it! Where on earth has the hot been connected to, then?
Norman The toilet cistern! That'll take a bit of sorting out, won't it? I rang because those plumbers have caused so much wasted time I just hope you haven't got them working on the factory complex too.
Peter No, no. They were sub-contractors. We certainly shan't be using *them* again.
Norman I'm glad to hear it.

connect join
defect mistake, fault
discover find
hang on a minute wait a minute (used especially on the telephone)
leak allow water to pass through where it shouldn't
manufacturer maker of products

occupy live in
sorting out putting right
sub-contractor *see* 0.1
tap head *see* fig. 119
toilet cistern *see* 7.6.b **cistern**
waste (shower waste, etc) waste fitting; *see* fig. 119

Answer the questions.

1 Who has Norman been talking to at the Cavendish Hotel?
2 Who was responsible for putting right the leaking shower wastes?
3 What is causing the problem this time?
4 How have the taps been connected up on the basin?
5 Why is there no hot in the bath?
6 Who is responsible for putting right the mistakes?

Fill in Sid's part of the conversation he had with Norman at the Cavendish Hotel.

Norman Hello, Sid. I just came down to see how everything was going.

Sid ....

Norman Oh, you mean the leaking shower wastes, do you?

Sid ....

Norman Well, shall we go and see for ourselves?

(*in the Manager's flat*)

Norman Try the bath first, Sid.

Sid ....

Norman Well, it won't be very hard to change those tap heads over. What about the basin?

Sid ....

Norman Try the toilet, then.

Sid ....

Norman Yes, it certainly will. Do you think Peter has got those plumbers working on the factory as well?

Sid ....

7.3.b Using the passive (perfect tense)

The passive is used when what has been done is more important than who has done it. Look at these sentences from the conversation:

The shower wastes *have* already *been seen to.*

Where . . . . . *has* the hot *been connected to?*

Here the passive is used in its perfect form (have/has been + past participle). Practise putting the correct form of the perfect passive into these sentences.

Example:
The contractor's work is not finished until the building (occupy) for several months.
The contractor's work is not finished until the building has been occupied for several months.

1 Many problems with the plumbing (discover) since work finished on the Cavendish Hotel.
2 The leaking shower wastes (fix) now.
3 What problem (find) in the Manager's flat?
4 The tap heads on the bath (fix) to the wrong taps.
5 The hot water from the basin (connect) to the toilet cistern.
6 A different firm of plumbers (give) the sub-contract for work on the factory complex.

Communication on Site

Reported speech: passing on what other people have said

7.4.a Reported statements

Look at these two speeches.

A   *Sid* (to Norman) 'We've found some problems with the plumbing at the Cavendish.'

B   *Norman* (to Peter) 'Sid says they've found some problems with the plumbing at the Cavendish.'

In A we have Sid's actual words to Norman (*direct* speech).
In B Norman is reporting to Peter what Sid has said (*indirect* or *reported* speech). Reported speech is used a lot on site to pass on what someone else has said. Look through conversation 7.3.a for some more examples. Try to imagine what Sid's actual words to Norman would have been.

Now let us look more carefully at how direct speech is changed when it is reported to someone else. Here are some examples.

Sid's actual words	Sid's words reported	
	Present tense (says)	Past tense (said)
The run's leaking a bit	Sid *says* the run's *leaking* a bit	Sid *said* the run *was leaking* a bit
I'll come and check it tomorrow	Sid *says* he'*ll come* and check it tomorrow	Sid *said* he *would come* and check it tomorrow
The others have been checked already	Sid *says* the others *have been checked* already	Sid *said* the others *had been checked* already

From the examples we see that when the reporting verb is present tense (Sid *says* . . .) then the reported speech stays in the same tense as the actual speech. But when the reporting verb is in the past tense (Sid *said*), then all present tense verbs change to past in the reported speech. Look through conversation 7.1.a for more examples of reported speech. Again, try to imagine what the original words would have been, this time remembering what we have said about tense changes.

Practise reporting these speeches, each time using a reporting verb first in the present tense and then in the past tense.

Example:
Bert I think there'll have to be some changes here.
Bert says he thinks there'll have to be some changes here.
Bert said he thought there would have to be some changes here.

1 **Keith** I think the screed will be 65 mm thick.
2 **Bert** I've already marked it in on the drawing.
3 **Alec** Sid's coming to check the reading this afternoon.
4 **Phil** You can often hear something when there's a leak.
5 **Norman** We've just been running all the taps.
6 **Peter** We won't be using those plumbers again.

141

7.4.b Reported questions

So far all the examples of reported speech we have talked about have been statements. Questions can also be reported. On site reported questions are often requests for information, or enquiries. Look at these examples:

Actual question	Reported question
Phil Are all the runs working all right now?	Phil wondered if (whether) all the runs were working all right now.
Keith How big are the pipes in here?	Keith was asking how big the pipes were in here.
Peter Where on earth has the hot been connected to?	Peter wants to know where the hot has been connected to.

You will see that if the actual question has a question word (how? where? etc), this is repeated in the reported question. If there is no question word we have to use 'if' or 'whether' after the reporting verb. Now look at this conversation:

Sid Has this run been checked yet?
Alex I'm not sure. I'll go and ask Phil.
(to Phil) Sid wants to know if that run has been checked yet.

Write conversations on this pattern, starting with each of these questions:

1 **Keith** Will you have to cross any of these conduits with your pipes?
  Bert ....
  (to electrician) ....
2 **Manager** Why can't I get any hot water in my bathroom?
  Peter ....
  (to plumber) ....
3 **Sid** Have all the pipes been lagged in here?
  Phil ....
  (to Alec) ....
4 **Manager** Who will be coming over to sort out these problems?
  Norman ....
  (to Peter) ....
5 **Peter** When will Bert be ready with his new pipe layout?
  Keith ....
  (to Bert) ....
6 **Sid** Are you going to test the two halves separately?
  Alec ....
  (to Phil) ....

7.4.c Reported instructions, advice, suggestions

Instructions, suggestions and advice can also be reported. There are many different ways of passing them on to someone else. Look at these examples.

Sid's actual words	Reported
Test the two halves separately	Sid *told us to* test the two halves separately.
	Sid *said to* test the two halves separately.

I think you ought to test . . .	Sid *thought we should* test . . .
	Sid *suggested we might* test . . .
You'd better test . . .	Sid *advised us to* test . . .
	Sid *said we'd better* test . . .

Practise passing on instructions, suggestions and advice to somebody else, using different expressions each time. You do not have to report the *exact* words in this exercise – just pass on the general idea of what has been said.

Example:

Resident Engineer Don't start laying your pipes until you've had a word with the electrician.

The resident engineer said not to start laying the pipes until we'd had a word with the electrician.

1 **Sid** You'd better trace that leak. The reading looks a bit high to me.

2 **Keith** Get it all sorted out on paper first and then check it with the resident engineer.

3 **Sid** You could try using a smoke test if you can't trace that leak with an air test.

4 **Norman** You must get those plumbers back to finish the job off properly.

5 **Sid** You must get the plumbing in here sorted out as soon as possible.

6 **Manager** Send somebody over at once – there's something wrong with the plumbing.

7.4.d Practice conversation

You can get more practise by rewriting conversation 7.2.a in reported speech. (Keith said . . . Bert told him . . . He wondered . . . Keith suggested . . . etc).

7.5 Drainage (52)

7.5.a Materials and Components

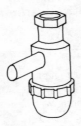

bottle trap

drain plug

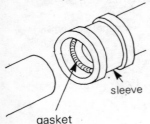

gasket | sleeve

asbestos cement pipe (52)If6 drain pipe made from asbestos cement
bottle trap (52.6) simple waste trap for use on a sink or basin
cast iron pipe (52.6)Ih1 drain pipe made from cast iron, sometimes used as a stack pipe
concrete pipe (52)If2 drain pipe made from concrete
down pipe (52.5)I rain water pipe (r.w.p.) fixed vertically to a wall
drain pipe (52)I pipe used to carry waste solids and liquids
drain plug (52.7) device which blocks a drain while tests or repairs are done
gasket ring of rubber or plastic used to seal a pipe joint
grating cover used in a gully
guard cage (52) fitting used at the top of a rainwater pipe or ventilating pipe to prevent objects from dropping into it
gully (52) drain trap into which waste water is discharged
pitch fibre pipe (52)Is1 drain pipe made from black, sticky material (tar), with wood or asbestos fibres, usually used below ground.
rodding eye (52) hole in a pipe with a cover which may be removed to clean the pipe
sleeve (52) push-fit drain pipe joint
stoneware g2 drain pipes and fittings made from clay, and often salt glazed
unplasticised polyvinyl (U.P.V.C.) n6 plastic used to make drain pipes and fittings
waste fitting (74) see fig. 119
yarn j3 fabric made from hemp, which is covered with tar and used to seal spigot and socket joints

grating

guard cage

gully

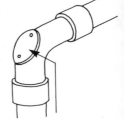

rodding eye

7.5.b Tools

air pressure gauge (B7) device to measure air pressure, used to test drains
clearing wheel (B8u) see fig. 112
double worm screw (B8u) see fig. 112
drain rods (B8u) lengths of wood or metal used to clean out drains; see fig. 112
drain testing plug see fig. 112
drop scraper (B8u) see fig. 112
pipe cutter (B5) see fig. 112
rod release key (B8u) see fig. 112
rubber plunger (B8u) see fig. 112

clearing wheel

double worm
screw

drop scraper

rubber plunger

drain rod

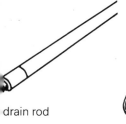

rod release key

drain testing plug

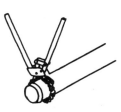

pipe cutter

fig 112 Drainage tools

7.5.c Actions

drain encased in
concrete

7.5.d General

drainlaying (D6) placing drains in trenches in the ground
encasing in concrete (D6) placing concrete all round a drain to
  protect it
lagging pipes (D6) fixing insulation around pipes
rodding drains (D7) cleaning out drains using drain rods
testing drains checking that drains do not leak
  1 **air test**: air is pumped into the drain
  2 **smoke test**: the drain is filled with smoke which has a strong smell
  3 **water test**: the drain is filled with water
backing up the filling up of a drain which is blocked, eg the sewage
  is backing up into the gully
benching (52.7) cement mortar used to build up the sides of a drain
  inside a manhole; see fig. 116
bend (52.7)I piece of curved pipe, eg quarter (¼) bend (90°); eighth
  (⅛) bend (135°)

bend

branch (52)I horizontal pipe which joins a vertical pipe, eg w.c.
  branch
combined drain (52.7)I drain which carries both foul sewage and
  surface water
deep seal trap (52) trap with a lot of water forming the seal
discharge (52.3) waste material which has to be removed from a
  sanitary appliance (fixture) such as a basin or w.c.

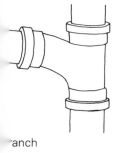

branch

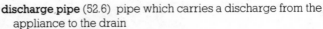

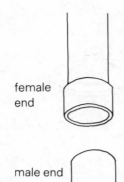

female end

male end

discharge pipe (52.6) pipe which carries a discharge from the appliance to the drain

drain (52.7)I pipe laid in the ground which carries waste material from a building to a sewer

easy bend (52)I large curve in a pipe which drain rods may pass through

fall the slope on a drain so that liquids (eg water) will flow through it, eg 1:20 fall; 1:100 fall

female the end of a pipe or fitting into which another one fits

foul water (52.3) waste water containing excreta or other unpleasant material

gradient fall

haunching concrete to support a drain

inspection chamber (52.7) point at which there is access to a drain to clean it out

invert level (52.7)I level taken at the bottom of a drain

male the end of a pipe or fitting which fits into another

manhole (52.7) deep inspection chamber with step irons into which a man may climb; see fig. 116

one-pipe system (52.6)I above ground drainage in a building in which all waste is discharged (run) into one vertical pipe; see fig. 114

seal see **water seal**

self-cleansing drain (52.6)I drain laid to a fall so that solids are carried along by the liquids

septic tank (52.7) large tank in the ground to collect sewage and drain away the water; see fig. 117

sewage (52.3) foul water

sewer (52.7)I large pipe to carry sewage, into which drains discharge

single stack system (52.6)I one-pipe system in which the stack itself is ventilated; see fig. 113

socket (52)I female end of a pipe

soil waste (52.3) foul waste

soil vent pipe (52.6)I the vertical pipe in a single stack system; see fig. 114

spigot (52.6)I the male end of a pipe

stack pipe (52.6)I vertical waste pipe; see fig. 113

step iron (52.7) metal foothold fixed to the side of a manhole; see fig. 116

storm water (52) surface water

surface water (52) rainwater from roofs, roads and paths

trap (52.5) device which prevents foul air from passing from a drain into a sanitary appliance (fitting) by means of a water seal

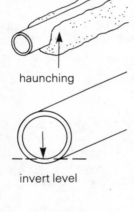

haunching

invert level

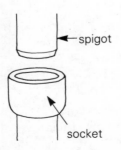

spigot

socket

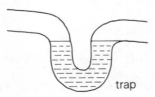

trap

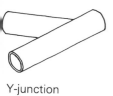

Y-junction

two-pipe system (52.6)I drainage system inside a building with two separate stack pipes; see fig. 115

ventilating pipe (52.6)I see fig. 115

waste pipe (52.6)I small pipe carrying waste water from a basin, bath or sink

water seal (52) water in a trap which stops air from passing through

Y-junction (52.7)I point at which a drain joins another drain.

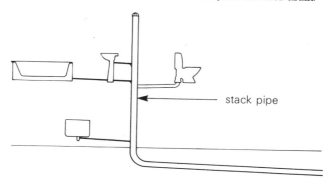

stack pipe

fig 113 **Single stack system of drainage**

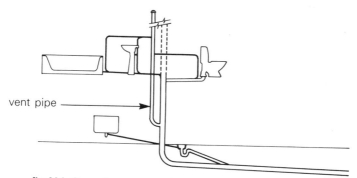

vent pipe

fig 114 **One-pipe system of drainage**

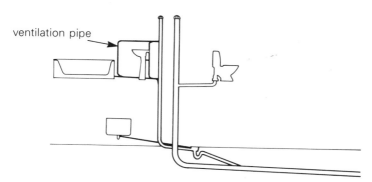

ventilation pipe

fig 115 **Two-pipe system of drainage**

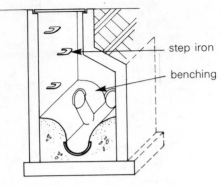

fig 116 **Manhole**

- step iron
- benching

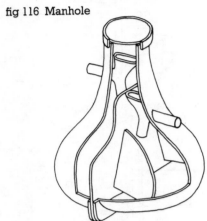

fig 117 **Septic tank**

7.6 Plumbing (5)

7.6.a Materials

tube of jointing paste

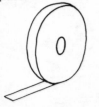

roll of jointing tape

acrylic n6 plastic used to make baths and basins

aluminium sheet h4 metal used for flashings (chemical formula Al)

brazing spelter h metal used to make a joint in brazing, made from copper (Cu) and zinc (Zn)

copper h6 metal used to make pipes, often used for water pipes (chemical formula Cu)

enamel v4 very hard surface finish applied to metals or stoneware

flux material used when making a soldered joint, eg tallow, resin, chloride of zinc, gallipoli oil, sal ammoniac

hemp j3 natural fibrous material used in a screwed joint to seal it

jointing paste t4 soft substance used in a screwed joint to seal it

jointing tape t4 thin plastic tape used in a screwed joint to seal it

lead h8 material used to make pipes (not now used very often), also much used in sheets for flashings (chemical formula Pb)

plastic n flexible material used to make pipes (which can be used as hot and cold water pipes) and plumbing fittings such as taps and stopcocks

porcelain g3 fine clay used as an enamel on cast iron products

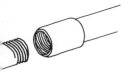

| screwed joint | solder (wire form) | solder (strip or rod form) | solder (granulated form) |

solder h soft metal which melts easily, used to make joints in metal pipes; solder is made from lead (Pb) and tin (Sn)

stainless steel h3 metal made from iron (Fe), with a smooth, clean surface, used to make pipes, sinks, and other sanitary fittings

steel h2 strong metal made from iron (Fe) used to make pipes, usually with screwed joints; steel pipes are used for gas and water

vitreous china g3 type of fine clay used to make basins and lavatory pans (w.c.s)

vitreous enamel v4 enamel made from glass

7.6.b Components **ball valve** (53) valve which stops water from going into a tank when it is full

cistern (53) water tank, eg tank for flushing w.c. (water closet)

combination tank (53) tank containing a hot water tank and a cold water tank with a ball valve

cylinder (53) hot water tank, usually made of copper

drain tap or **drain cock** (5_)I tap by which pipework may be emptied of water

expansion pipe (5_)I see fig. 124

expansion tank (5_)I see fig. 124

fitting (53) see fig. 119

hose reel (68.5) kind of wheel on which a fire hose is stored

joint (5_)I see fig. 125

lagging jacket (53) insulated cover for a water tank to keep heat in the tank or to stop the water from freezing

pipe (5_)I tube used to carry liquids and gases

pipe fixing (5_)I see fig. 121

pipe joint (5_)I see fig. 125

sanitary appliance (74) see fig. 120

stop cock or **stop tap** (5_)I tap which stops water flowing in a pipe

tap (53) device which controls the flow of water out of a pipe; see fig. 119

valve (53) device which controls the flow of water within a pipe, eg stop valve or stop cock

 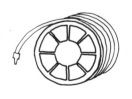 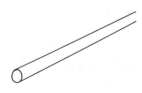

| cylinder | hose reel | pipe |

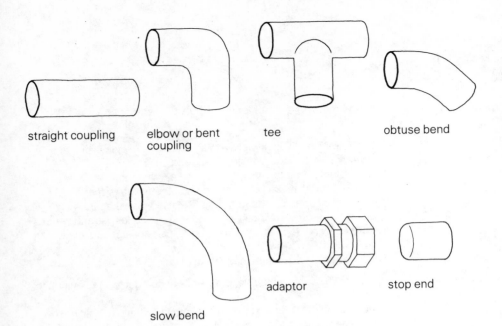

straight coupling

elbow or bent coupling

tee

obtuse bend

slow bend

adaptor

stop end

fig 118 Plumbing joint fittings

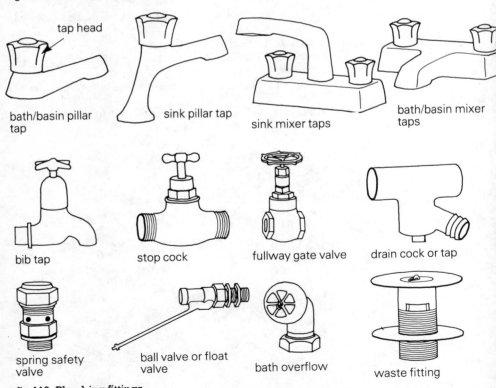

tap head

bath/basin pillar tap

sink pillar tap

sink mixer taps

bath/basin mixer taps

bib tap

stop cock

fullway gate valve

drain cock or tap

spring safety valve

ball valve or float valve

bath overflow

waste fitting

fig 119 Plumbing fittings

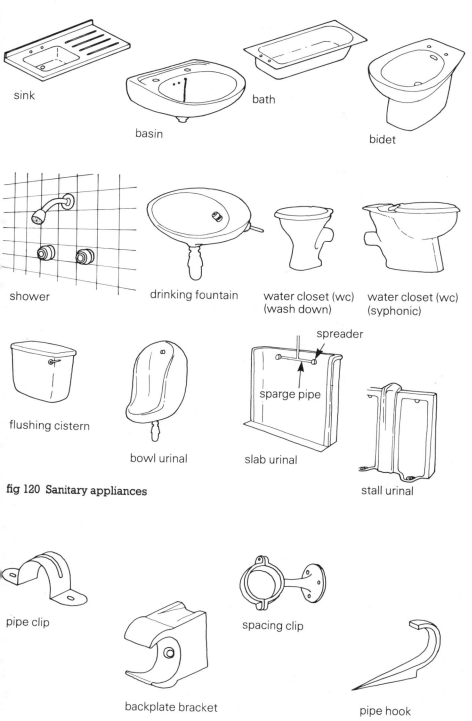

sink

basin

bath

bidet

shower

drinking fountain

water closet (wc)
(wash down)

water closet (wc)
(syphonic)

flushing cistern

bowl urinal

spreader

sparge pipe

slab urinal

stall urinal

fig 120 Sanitary appliances

pipe clip

backplate bracket

spacing clip

pipe hook

fig 121 Pipe fixings

basin wrench (B7) see fig. 122

blow torch or **blow lamp** (B7) tool which burns paraffin or gas to give a hot flame; see fig. 122

bending spring (B7) long object made from metal wire which is put inside a pipe before bending it; see fig. 122

burring reamer (B5) see fig. 122

caulking tool (B7) tool for pushing lead into a caulked joint

cold chisel (B7) see fig. 123

floorboard chisel (B7) see fig. 123

force cup (B7) see fig. 122

hacksaw (B7) see fig. 123

oxy-acetylene torch (B7) very hot blow lamp which burns oxygen and acetylene

pipe-bending machine (B7) see fig. 122

pipe wrench (B7) see fig. 122

plumb and level(B7) tool to check that pipe is horizontal or vertical

rasp (B7 see fig. 123

shave hook (B7) see fig. 123

sledge hammer (B7) see fig. 123

soldering iron (B7) see fig. 122

spanner (B7) tool for tightening nuts

steel wool (B7) strands of steel used to clean pipework before making a joint

stillson wrench (B7) see fig. 122

stocks and dies (B5) tools for cutting threads into steel pipes

tank cutter (B7) see fig. 122

tin snips (B7) tool for cutting sheet metal

wiping cloth (B7) piece of moleskin used for making a wiped soldered joint

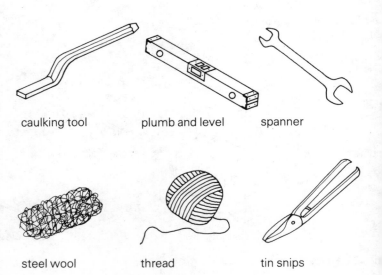

caulking tool   plumb and level   spanner

steel wool   thread   tin snips

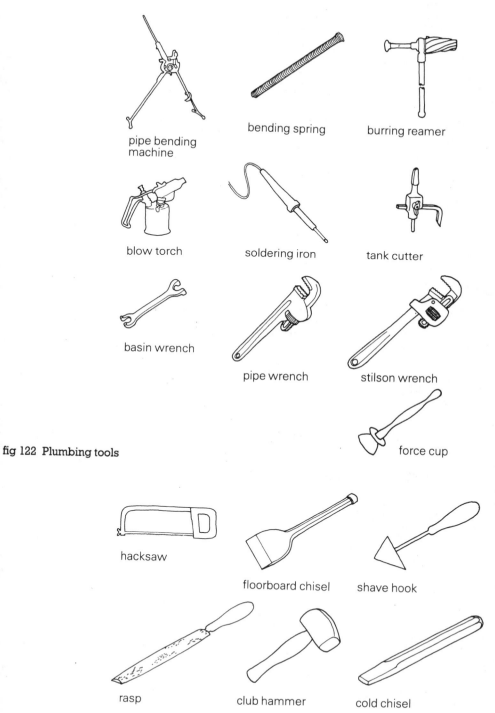

bending spring

burring reamer

pipe bending
machine

blow torch

soldering iron

tank cutter

basin wrench

pipe wrench

stilson wrench

force cup

fig 122 Plumbing tools

hacksaw

floorboard chisel

shave hook

rasp

club hammer

cold chisel

fig 123 Tools

brazing (B5) forming joints in pipework using brass spelter; brass is a metal containing copper (Cu) and zinc (Zn)

caulking a joint (B5) pushing lead or other material into a spigot and socket joint

dry fluxing (B5) putting powdered flux on to a joint

hard soldering (B5) brazing

preparing a joint (B5) cutting, shaping, cleaning, fluxing and clamping pipes before making a joint

soft soldering (B5) soldering using lead solder which melts easily

sweating a joint (B5) heating a capillary joint so that the solder runs inside it

tapping a water main (B5) cutting into a water main and fixing a new pipe while the water main is full of water

wet fluxing (B5) putting flux which has been mixed into a paste on a joint

air lock air in pipework which is difficult to get out

burst pipe (5_)I pipe broken by frost (very cold weather)

chase channel cut in a wall or floor

cover flashing (47) see fig. 126

dead leg (5_)I length of pipe which supplies one fitting only; long dead legs should be avoided

direction of flow (5_)I the way in which water runs in a pipe

distribution pipe (53)I see fig. 124

drencher system (68.5) system of water pipes used on the outside of large buildings to put out fires

dry riser (58) vertical pipe in a building which supplies fire fighting appliances; the pipe is empty until it is needed

flashing (47) metal sheet used to keep water out of roof junctions; see fig. 126

frost damage (5_)I pipework broken by ice in very cold weather

furring (5_)I material formed inside pipes used for hard water

hard water water containing chemical salts

head of water see fig. 124

lagging (5_)I insulation materials for pipes and tanks

pipe joint (5_)I see figs. 118 and 125 for various types

rising main (53)I vertical water main pipe in a building

service pipe (53)I see fig. 124

soaker (47) see fig. 126

soft water water containing few chemical salts

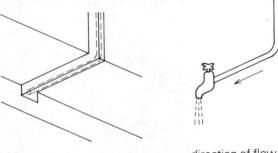

chase   direction of flow

sprinkler system(68.5) system of water pipes used in large buildings to put out fires

step flashing (47) see fig. 126

water hammer (53)I noise made in water pipes

water main (53)I pipe which brings cold water into a building; see fig. 124

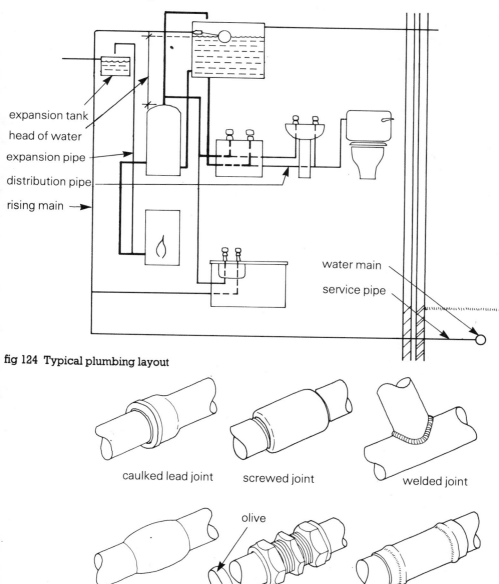

fig 124 Typical plumbing layout

expansion tank
head of water
expansion pipe
distribution pipe
rising main

water main
service pipe

caulked lead joint   screwed joint   welded joint

olive

wiped soldered joint   compression joint   capillary joint

fig 125 Plumbing joints

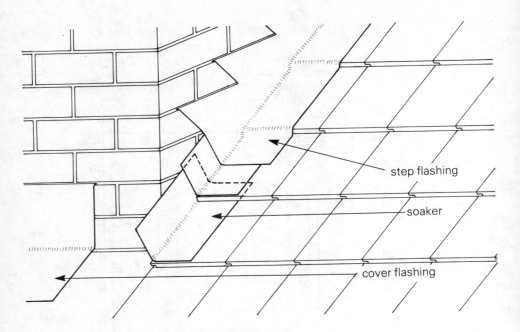

fig 126 Flashings

8 Heating, Ventilation and Electrical Services

Language Practice

8.1.a Heating

'Whose fault?'
Problems in a building may be the result of poor design or of poor workmanship or installation. Sometimes it is difficult to decide which is the cause.

fig 127

Cliff – *Services Engineer*
Mr Barton – *Heating Sub-contractor's Representative*

Cliff Well, you can hear the hum quite clearly in this room, you see. And this is some distance from the plant room, as you know.
Mr Barton Hmm. And yet we've just been round and checked all the boilers and circulating pumps. They're all operating fine.
Cliff Yes, they do seem to be. You know, I'm certain there must be something wrong with the pipework or the heating units.
Mr Barton I can't understand it. We've used exactly the same components before – boilers, pumps, pipework and convector units. We've never had any trouble at all. I suppose it couldn't be anything to do with the way the building has been designed, could it?
Cliff Well, it's not a lightweight building, you know. The sound insulation between rooms is really excellent.

Mr Barton Well, what do you suggest? As far as I can see the system's working perfectly – apart from this noise, that is.

Cliff Hmm . . .

Mr Barton We've installed it exactly as it was designed, and we've followed all the manufacturer's instructions. I just don't see what more we can do. Can you think of anywhere else we might have gone wrong?

Cliff No, I'm afraid not. I had another look at the heating design just now, but I couldn't see anything wrong with that either. We may have to call in the manufacturers of the boilers and pumps. But I really think we should make more tests first.

Mr Barton Yes, I suppose we ought to. Look, I'll send my foreman along tomorrow – he'll probably be able to help.

Cliff Okay, I'll meet him here at half-past eight in the morning.

boiler *see* 8.6.a
circulating pump *see* 8.6.a
component part
convector unit *see* 8.6.a
   convector heater
heating unit heat emitter
   see 8.6.a
hum continuous low noise
installation fitting components

lightweight building building made of light materials
manufacturer maker of products
operate work
pipework pipes; *see* 7.6.b
plant room room in which services machinery is fitted
workmanship quality of work

Answer the questions

1 What have Cliff and Mr Barton been doing? Why?
2 What does Cliff think must be wrong?
3 What sort of sound insulation does the building give?
4 Why may they have to call in the manufacturers?
5 What are they going to do first?
6 Who is Mr Barton going to send along in the morning?

Cliff is telling Peter, the site agent, about Mr Barton's site visit. Complete the sentences.

Mr Barton came today to .... He couldn't understand what had gone wrong because .... He wondered whether .... , but I told him .... So we've decided to .... and if we can't find anything ourselves .... we'll just have to ....

8.1.b 'Some' and 'any'

Look at these sentences from the conversation:

A   This is *some* distance from the plant room.
    There must be *something* wrong with the pipework.

    We've never had *any* trouble at all.
B   I couldn't see *anything* wrong with that, either.
    Can you think of *anywhere* else we might have gone wrong?

The A sentences are *statements without negatives* (not, never, nowhere, etc). Here we use 'some' words (some, somewhere, somebody, etc).
The B sentences are *questions* or *negatives*, and here we use 'any' words instead.
Choose the correct word to complete the sentences in this exercise.

Example:
Could there be a defect . . . . . in the heating circuit? (somewhere, anywhere)
Could there be a defect *anywhere* in the heating circuit?

1 Perhaps there's . . . . . wrong with the heating design. (something, anything)
2 Is there . . . . . sound insulation between the rooms here? (some, any)
3 Nobody has been able to find . . . . . wrong with the installation as yet. (something, anything)
4 Do you know . . . . . who might be able to help? (someone, anyone)
5 Before we ring the manufacturer, we'd better make . . . . . more tests. (some, any)
6 I'll send . . . . . along in the morning to help you, (someone, anyone)

8.2.a Ventilation   *'A building is an assembly of parts'*
Installation of a complicated air conditioning system using many components is a job which needs to be well organised.

fig 128

Terry – *Ductwork Installer*   Alan – *Apprentice Ductwork Installer*

Terry Now then, Alan, just have a look at this drawing a moment, will you? This is the ductwork we'll be fitting in the plant room, right?
Alan Oh yes.
Terry We've got the actual ductwork down here already, but all the smaller parts we'll be needing are still in the store.
Alan Oh.

Terry I'll just explain what all these are, shall I? Then I'd like you to go and fetch them. Okay?

Alan Oh, right.

Terry Now, look at that symbol there – that's a duct-mounted silencer. Do you know what it looks like? – it's a sort of metal cylindrical thing.

Alan Hmm.

Terry This one here – this is a fire damper made from intumescent material. It's flat and round. Have you ever seen one? It looks a bit like honeycomb.

Alan Oh, yes.

Terry And that one is a length of flexible ducting, and there's a constant flow rate controller valve.

Alan Hmm. Right.

Terry Are you listening, Alan? You don't seem to be paying much attention.

Alan Sorry, Terry. Actually, er – I was just wondering . . . would you mind if I left a bit early this afternoon?

Terry Well, there's a lot to do today. We've got to get all this ductwork up by the end of the afternoon, you know. Is it important?

Alan Well – my brother's in hospital. I was hoping to go and see him straight from work.

Terry Hmm. I wouldn't mind you leaving early sometimes if you got here on time in the mornings. Look, I'll tell you what. Let's see how the work goes today. You'd better try and make a good start this morning. If you get on okay, I'll let you go early this afternoon.

Alan Oh, thanks, Terry. Well, I'd better get started then. What would you like me to do first?

Terry Let's see, now. You go through the drawing and make yourself a list of all these parts we need. And if there's anything you don't understand, just let me know.

air conditioning *see* 8.7.b
assembly fitting together
complicated difficult to install
constant flow rate controller
  valve *see* 8.7.a
cylindrical in the form of a
  cylinder
duct-mounted
  silencer attenuator; *see* 8.7.a
ductwork *see* 8.7.a **duct**

fire damper *see* 8.7.a
flexible ducting *see* fig. 142
honeycomb hexagonal pattern
intumescent *see* 8.7.a
organise manage, plan
store *see* 1.5.a
symbol sign on a drawing
  representing a component or
  material

Answer the questions.

1 What does the drawing show?
2 What is Alan going to fetch from the store?
3 What does a fire damper look like? What is it made of?
4 What does Terry want to get done by the end of the afternoon?
5 What is Alan hoping to do straight from work?
6 Why is Alan going to make a list?

cylinder

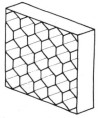

honeycomb

Fill in the blanks.

Terry and Alan are working on ....

.... has been brought down already but some of the smaller parts are still in the store, such as ....

Alan is hoping to leave work early because .... ,

but Terry wants to .... before they go home.

Alan's first job is ....

8.2.b 'If' clauses (past tense)

Look at these sentences from the conversation:

Would you *mind* if I *left* a bit early?

I *wouldn't mind* you leaving early . . . if you *got* here on time in the mornings.

These sentences are conditional sentences using 'if' (see also 1.2.b). When the verb in the 'if' clause is simple past tense, we use the conditional tense in the main clause (would/should + verb).

Here is an exercise to practise 'if' sentences with the past tense.

Example:

If you (arrive) on time we (get) more work done.

If you arrived on time we would get more work done.

---

1 If you (listen) to what I was saying, you (know) what to do.

2 I (not mind) you asking for time off if you (arrive) in good time.

3 If you (go) to see your brother you (have to) leave half an hour early.

4 I (let) you leave early if you (make) a good start on the ductwork.

5 It (be) easier if you (go) through the drawings and made a list first.

6 If you (bring) all those parts down here I (be able) to explain what they all were.

8.3.a Electrical Services

'Taking a risk'

Electricity is a big danger on a building site, and many electricians take risks to save a few minutes of their time.

Wilfred – *Foreman Electrician*   Julian – *Electrician*   (Mr Hamilton – *Safety Officer*)

Julian Oh hello, Wilfred. You know, I'm still having trouble with these washing-up machines. I can't get them to work at all. You'll have to see if you can find what's wrong.

fig 129

Wilfred Right. Well, we know we've got power, anyway, so there's nothing wrong with the wiring. Have you had a chance to check that fuse?

Julian Yes, I've just changed it, so it must be all right.

Wilfred Oh. Well, there's only one other thing it could be really. That isolator switch must be faulty or something.

Julian Do you think so? Well, I can easily change that. Here, lend me your screwdriver a minute and I'll fit the other one.

Wilfred You'd better not, you know! Have you forgotten the juice is still on?

Julian Well, that's all right, isn't it? I've done it before, Wilfred.

Wilfred Not to my knowledge you haven't. You're not to risk it, do you hear? Don't you let me see you working on live appliances.

Julian All right, then.

Wilfred Well, surely it's not much trouble to switch off first, is it?

Julian All right, all right, I'm sorry – I didn't realise you felt so strongly about it.

Wilfred Well, I do. Anyway, it's not just me, you know. Mr Hamilton is always telling me about it. He's always saying 'Wilfred, don't let any of your men take any chances with live electricity, because if anyone has an accident we'll both be out of a job.'

appliance piece of equipment
faulty not working
fuse *see* 8.5.a
isolator switch *see* 8.5.a
juice electrician's name for electricity
live connected to electric supply

power supply of electricity
risk chance, dangerous course of action
screwdriver *see* 8.5.b
wiring *see* 8.5.d

Answer the questions.
1 What is the trouble with the washing-up machines?
2 What have they checked already?
3 What does Wilfred think must be the cause of the trouble?

4 What is Julian going to do with the screwdriver?
5 Why is he taking a risk?
6 What does Mr Hamilton say about working with electricity?

Complete Julian's part of the conversation.
Wilfred How are you getting on now, Julian?
Julian ....
Wilfred Oh dear. Well, are you getting power through all right?
Julian ....
Wilfred Have you checked the fuse yet?
Julian ....
Wilfred Yes, I think it must be. You'd better change it.
Julian ....
Wilfred Just a minute – have you switched off yet?
Julian ....
Wilfred Well, you'd better make sure you don't do it again. You know
what Mr Hamilton's always saying, don't you?
Julian ....
Wilfred That's right. And I don't want to lose my job. So don't do it
again.

8.3.b Irregular verbs
English is full of common irregular verbs. Here is a list of some of the
most useful ones. (You can find several of these used in the
conversation.) Check through the list now and make sure you know
all the different forms of each verb.

Verb	A Simple Past		B Present Perfect
bring	brought		brought
come	came		come
do	did		done
find	found		found
forget	forgot		forgotten
get	got		got
go	went	(have/has)	gone
know	knew		known
let	let		let
make	made		made
say	said		said
see	saw		seen
take	took		taken
think	thought		thought

To practise these irregular verbs, put the verbs in these sentences
into the simple past tense (A) or the present perfect (B). *Don't* look at
the list as you do this exercise – *cover it over!*

Example:

Wilfred (come: A) to see how
Julian was getting on
Wilfred came to see how Julian
was getting on.

Wilfred (come: B) to see how
Julian is getting on.
Wilfred has come to see how
Julian is getting on.

163

1 They (not find: B) anything wrong with the wiring.
2 Julian (know: A) there was nothing wrong with the fuse.
3 Wilfred (think: A) the isolator switch was faulty.
4 Julian (forget: B) to switch off the juice.
5 Wilfred (see: A) Julian working on a live appliance.
6 Mr Hamilton (say: A) never to take any chances.

Communication on Site

Permission, obligation and prohibition

8.4.a Permission

Sometimes on site you may have to ask whether you are allowed to do something, or whether it is all right for you to do something at a certain time. This is asking for permission. Look at conversation 8.2.a where Alan is asking for permission to leave work early. How does he do this? Some other ways he might ask are:

Is it all right if I leave early?
Do you think I could leave early today?
Can I/May I leave early this afternoon?
Please could I leave early today?
I wonder if I could leave early this afternoon?
Do you mind if I leave early tonight?

Terry might give him permission like this:

Sure, that would be okay.
Yes, that's fine.
Yes, you may.
Yes, all right.
Yes, I should think so.
No, I don't mind at all.

Practise asking for permission, and giving it, in this exercise. Write a short conversation in the example pattern for each situation, and try to use different expressions every time.

Example:
Alan would like to go and fetch his cigarettes. (Terry)
Alan Do you think I could just go and get my cigarettes, Terry?
Terry Sure, that'll be all right.

---

1 Mr Barton would like to use the office telephone. (Peter)
2 Julian would like to have the afternoon off tomorrow. (Wilfred)
3 Alan would like to start work about an hour late on Thursday. (Terry)
4 Mr Hamilton would like to come and check over the wiring later on. (Wilfred)
5 Alan would like to take his lunch-break half an hour earlier than usual. (Terry)
6 Cliff would like to make a suggestion. (Mr Barton)

Sometimes when we ask for permission we feel we have to give a reason (see 3.4.a). What is Alan's reason for wanting to leave early in conversation 8.2.a? We often feel we have to give reasons, too, when we won't give our permission for something. What reasons does Terry give for not wanting Alan to leave early?

8.4.b Obligation

As well as finding out whether we are *allowed* to do something, we might sometimes be told that we have *got* to do something – or *ought* to do it. This is called obligation.

We have several ways of expressing obligation in English. We use 'must' or 'have (got) to' when it is absolutely necessary to do something:

> You *must* finish this by lunchtime.
> We'll *have to* call in the manufacturers.
> We've *got to* get all this ductwork up by the end of the afternoon.

We use 'should' or 'ought to' for an obligation which is not necessarily going to be fulfilled:

> I really think we *should* make more tests first. (but perhaps you won't agree)
> You *ought to* finish this before you leave. (but you might not manage it)

We use 'had better' for the best or most advisable thing to do:

> You'd *better* try and make a good start this morning.
> You'd *better* remember to switch the juice off next time.

In this exercise, make up three sentences for each situation to practise using the three kinds of obligation we have described.

Example:

(Alan) Look at the drawing more carefully next time.
Alan *must* look at the drawing more carefully next time.
Alan *ought to* look at the drawing more carefully next time.
Alan *had better* look at the drawing more carefully next time.

---

1 (We) Make some more tests today.
2 (The men) Switch off the current for this job.
3 (You) Tell Julian not to take any chances with live electricity.
4 (You) Go through the drawing and make yourself a list.
5 (Alan) Try to get here on time if he wants to leave early.
6 (We) Call in the manufacturers of the boilers.

8.4.c Prohibition

Prohibition is sometimes the refusal of permission to do something. Look at these answers to the question '*Is it all right if I go early?*'

> You can't today, I'm afraid.
> I'm sorry, but it's not possible/convenient.
> No, I don't think so.
> I'm afraid not.

Prohibition can also be an obligation *not* to do something.

> You mustn't switch on until I say.
> You're not to risk it.
> You mustn't start putting up the ductwork until I come.

We can also express prohibition in imperatives (see 2.2.b).

> Don't switch on yet!
> Don't go until you've finished the ductwork.

Can you find some more examples of this kind of prohibition in conversation 8.3.a?

8.4.d Practice Conversations

Now practise writing conversations using prohibition in these situations.

Words you will need:
current see 8.5.d
distribution board see 8.5.a
switch room room containing electrical distribution equipment

1 Wilfred comes into the switch room. Julian has taken the cover off the distribution board and is looking to see what work needs to be done on it. Wilfred asks whether the current has been switched off and Julian says no. Wilfred tells him to switch off at once. He says the board is so dangerous that Julian must never touch it when the current is on, even if he is only taking the cover off to have a look. Write the conversation which you imagine takes place between Wilfred and Julian. Begin your conversation like this:

Wilfred *Ah, hello, Julian. So you've started on the distribution board already, have you?*

2 Terry asks Alan why he has fitted a duct-mounted silencer (see wordlist 8.2.a) in a different position from where the drawing indicates. Alan says it was much easier to put the silencer there than where the drawing showed. Terry says Alan must change the position of the silencer because now it doesn't comply with the specification. Alan says he doesn't think the new position will make any difference, but Terry says he will have to change it all the same. He tells Alan he must not make any changes in the specification without first checking to make sure it is all right. Write the conversation between Terry and Alan, beginning like this:

Terry *Why has this silencer been fitted in the wrong place, Alan?*

Reference Section

8.5 Electrical (6_)

8.5.a Materials and Components

alarm bell (68.5) electric bell used as a fire bell or burglar alarm
armoured cable (61) cable covered with metal for use underground
battery (62) device which stores electricity
bayonet fitting (63) type of fixing for a light bulb
bell (64) device which makes a loud ringing noise, eg doorbell
buckle clip (61)t6 clip to fix wiring

battery

bayonet fitting

bell

buckle clip

cartridge fuse

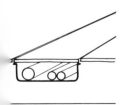
flexible metal
trunking

floor trunking
(section)

burglar alarm (68.2) security bell to warn of thieves
bus bar (61) metal rod used to conduct large electrical currents
within a building
cable (61) see fig. 134 for various types
cartridge fuse (61) fuse wire enclosed in a case
ceiling rose (63) see fig. 132
circuit breaker (61) device which cuts out an electrical supply if
there is a fault, eg earth leakage circuit breaker
cooker point (62) see fig. 132
conduit box (61) see fig. 135
consumer unit (61) box containing a main switch and fuses; see
fig. 132
copper metal (chemical formula Cu) often used to make electrical
cable
distribution board (61) see fig. 132
double pole switch (61) switch which breaks the live and neutral
lines when off
electric fan (61) see 8.6.a **fan**
electricity meter (61) device which measures the amount of
electricity being used in a building
electric motor (61) device which uses electricity to produce motion
(movement), eg an electric fan contains an electric motor
escalator (61) moving staircase
filament (63) see fig. 133
fire alarm (68.5) system of bells or sirens to give warning of fire
flex (61) wire; see fig. 134
flexible metal trunking (61) duct which will bend
floor trunking (61) channel in a floor to contain electrical wiring
fuse (61) length of wire in an electrical circuit which blows (breaks) if
the circuit is overloaded

gland

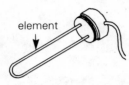

element

immersion heater

light bulb

screw fitting

generator (61) machine which produces electricity

gland (61) ring which protects a cable as it enters a fitting

isolator (61) large switch which cuts off an electrical supply

immersion heater (61) electric water heater used in a hot water cylinder

incandescent lamp (63) filament lamp; see fig. 133

lamp (63) source of electric light; light bulbs and light fittings are called lamps

lift (61) see fig. 136

light bulb (63) lamp

light fitting (63) see fig. 130 for various types

lightning conductor (61) strip of metal fixed to the outside of a building from top to bottom and taken to earth

luminaire (63) light fitting

mineral insulated copper covered (MICC) cable (61) see fig. 134

miniature circuit breaker (MCB) (61) circuit breaker which may be used in an electrical circuit instead of a fuse

meter cabinet (61) box with a door in which an electric meter may be fixed, often used for a house

meter tails (61) cable running from a meter to a consumer unit or distribution board

oval conduit (61) plastic conduit for electrical wiring: see fig. 135

plug or plugtop (62) see fig. 132

power point (62) socket outlet; see fig. 132

quartz-halogen bulb (63) tungsten-halogen bulb

relay (61) switch operated by an electric current

rising main (61) mains electricity cable fixed vertically within a building

screw fitting (63) type of fixing for a light bulb

service cable (61) cable between an electricity main (outside a building) and the electricity meter inside the building; see fig. 138

skirting trunking (61) duct for electrical wiring fixed at low level instead of a skirting board

smoke detector (68.5) device which makes an alarm bell ring when there is smoke in the air

sodium lamp (63) kind of bulb giving an orange light

socket outlet (62) see fig. 132

spur box (61) see fig. 132

switch (61) see fig. 131 for various types

switch box (61) see fig. 131

switch fuse (61) switch which contains a fuse

time clock (61) electric clock which puts a switch on or off at certain times

track lighting (63) see fig. 130

transformer (61) device which reduces the voltage of an electric current

trunking (61) metal duct in which electrical wiring is laid within a building

tungsten halogen lamp (63) very bright electric light bulb

wire (61) length of metal which conducts electricity; see fig. 134

lamp holder   pendant fitting   fluorescent lighting

floodlight   spotlight   downlighter

recessed luminaire   track lighting

fig 130 Light fittings

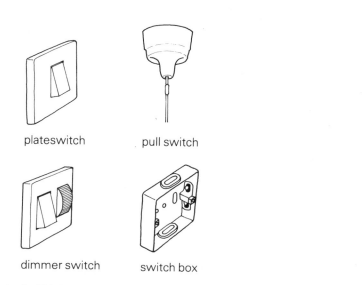

plateswitch   pull switch

dimmer switch   switch box

fig 131 Electrical switches

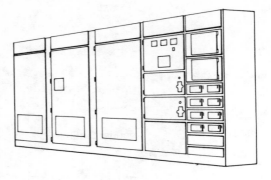

distribution board

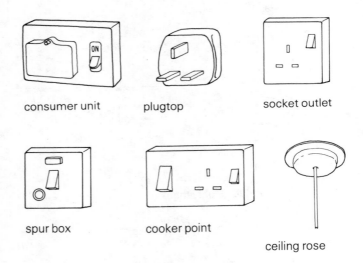

consumer unit   plugtop   socket outlet

spur box   cooker point

ceiling rose

fig 132 Electrical equipment and fittings

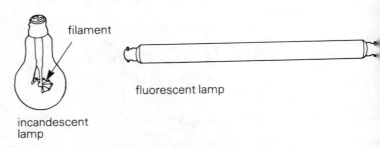

filament

incandescent
lamp

fluorescent lamp

fig 133 Electric lamps

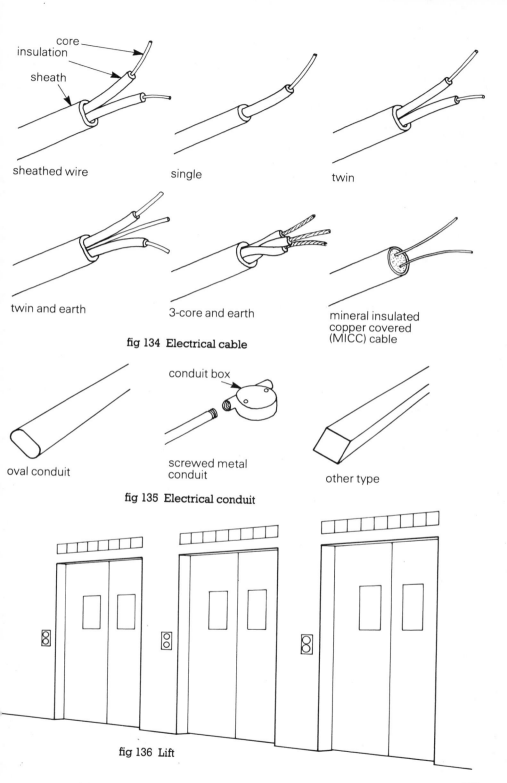

core
insulation
sheath

sheathed wire

single

twin

twin and earth

3-core and earth

mineral insulated
copper covered
(MICC) cable

fig 134 Electrical cable

oval conduit

conduit box

screwed metal
conduit

other type

fig 135 Electrical conduit

fig 136 Lift

multimeter

ammeter (B8v) meter which measures an electric current in amps
multimeter (B8v) general purpose measuring meter for testing electrical work
pliers (B7) (pair of pliers) tool which can strip and cut electrical wire
screwdriver (B7) tool for tightening screws
step ladder ladder which stands on its own
voltmeter (B8v) meter which measures the potential difference of a supply of electricity, in volts
wire cutters (B7) tool for cutting electrical wire
wire strippers (B7) tool for removing the insulation from electrical wiring

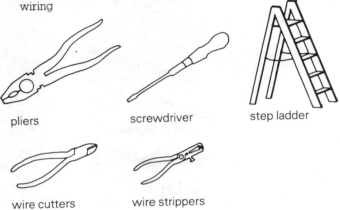

pliers   screwdriver   step ladder

wire cutters   wire strippers

connecting up (D7) joining an electrical installation to the mains electricity supply
drilling a joist (D4) making a hole in a timber joist for a wire to pass through
earthing an installation (D6) fixing wires buried into the ground at one end, which make an electrical installation safe
installing electrical equipment (D6) fixing in place electrical appliances, light fittings and wiring

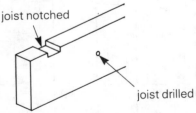

joist notched

joist drilled

notching a joist (D4) cutting the top or bottom of a timber joist for a wire to pass through
stripping wire (D4) removing the insulation material (usually plastic) from the end of a piece of electrical wire
wiring a building (D6) fixing electrical wiring in a building
wiring up an appliance (D6) fixing wiring to a fitting which needs a supply of electricity

stripped wire

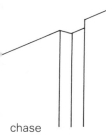

chase

alternating current (AC) type of current normally supplied on a mains supply

cable rating the largest electrical current which may pass through a cable safely

chase channel cut in a wall

circuit closed path around which an electric current can flow

colour code colours used for different kinds of wires in a cable, eg brown for live, blue for neutral and green/yellow for earth

conductor material which conducts (carries) electricity easily, eg copper (Cu) is a good conductor

current flow of electricity in a circuit

direct current (DC) type of current supplied by a battery

earth the ground, where an electric current flows to if it can

earth leakage passing of a current to earth from a circuit

electric shock passing of a current to earth through a person's body

emergency lighting (63.8) lights which come on when the mains electricity supply goes off

installation all of the electrical control equipment (switches, fuses), wiring and appliances (lights, fans, heaters) which are installed in a building

insulator material which does not conduct electricity easily, eg plastic is a good insulator

intake (61) the electricity supply, measured in kilowatts (kW) which is fed into a building

kilowatt (kW) one thousand watts (1,000 W)

live positive (+) terminal or wire in a circuit; also, any wire with a current passing through it is said to be 'live'

loop-in method of wiring (6_) see fig. 137

maintained lighting (63.8) lights normally run by a mains supply, and which stay on when the mains supply goes off

negative (– or –ve) battery terminal connected to the neutral line

neutral negative (–) terminal or wire in a circuit

neon light red light caused by passing electricity through neon (Ne) gas

non-maintained lighting (63.8) emergency lights which are not used unless the mains supply goes off

overloading running too much current through a circuit, causing the fuse to blow

positive (+ or +ve) battery terminal connected to a live line

public address (P.A.) (64.3) system of microphones, amplifier and loudspeakers in a building

ring circuit or **ring main** (6_) see fig. 138

security system (68.2) alarm bells which can be set to ring if a building is broken into by burglars

self-contained light (63.8) emergency light with its own battery, which may be re-charged from the mains supply

short circuit

short circuit circuit in which the live and neutral wires are connected by mistake, causing a fuse to blow

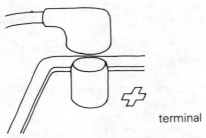

terminal

stand-by power (63.8) supply of electricity (often batteries) used to
run emergency lighting

terminal point at which a wire is connected to a battery or appliance

three (3) phase supply (61) usual type of supply to large buildings

volt (V) measure of potential difference in a supply; British mains
supply is 240V

voltage drop voltage made smaller in a circuit with long wires

watt (W) measure of electrical power

wiring (61) electrical wires in an installation

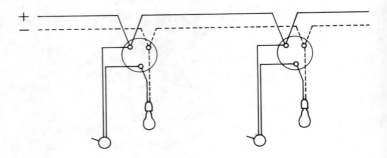

fig 137 **Loop-in method of wiring**

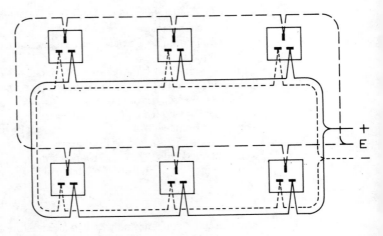

fig 138 **Ring circuit**

8.6 Heating (56)

8.6.a Materials and Components

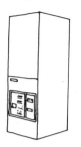

combination boiler

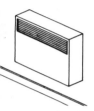

convector heater

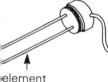

element

micro-bore pipe

air curtain (56.8) warm air blown from above an entrance door

anti-vibration mounting (5_) flexible support (eg made from rubber) for a machine to prevent noise and movement from being carried around the building

back boiler (56.1) water heater fixed behind a room heater, to heat radiators and supply domestic hot water

balanced flue (56.1) flue which passes through an external wall behind a boiler

boiler (56.1) device which burns fuel to produce heat; fuel may be solid fuel, oil or gas

burner (56.1) part of a gas or oil boiler where the fuel burns

calorifier (56) heat exchanger

circulating pump (56) device (usually electric) which makes hot water run through pipes and radiators

combination boiler (56) boiler containing a water heater and hot and cold water storage tanks

convector heater (56) heater which makes currents of warm air

element (56) part of an electric water or space heater which gets hot

flue (56) duct which carries burnt gases from a boiler up into the air outside the building

gas substance which is not solid or liquid; eg air contains several gases

heat emitter (56) device such as a radiator which becomes warm and gives out heat

heat exchanger (56) device which passes heat from one circulation system to another, eg an indirect hot water cylinder

heat pump (56) device which can take heat at low temperature from air, water or earth; refrigeration plant is a kind of heat pump

neat source (56) boiler or other heater supplying a heating system

micro-bore pipe (56.3) very small pipe used for high pressure hot water (HPHW) heating

oil (5.1) heating fuel made from petroleum

radiant heater (56) heater which gives off radiant heat, ie like heat from the sun

radiator (56) type of heat emitter; see fig. 139 for various types

radiator valve (56) tap to switch a radiator on and off, or to balance it

sectional boiler (56.1) boiler which is made of several parts bolted together; often made of cast iron

sectional boiler

solar collector flat panel which takes in heat from the sun

solar panel solar collector

small bore pipe (56.3) pipe approximately 15 mm diameter used in low pressure hot water (LPHW) heating

solid fuel (5.1) coal, coke, wood, peat or other material which may be burned for heat

storage heater (56) electric heater which heats up during the night and stores heat

thermostat (56) switch which goes off and on as the temperature in a room rises and falls

thermostatic radiator valve (TRV) (56) radiator tap which acts as a thermostat

union valve (56) stopcock fixed either side of a circulating pump

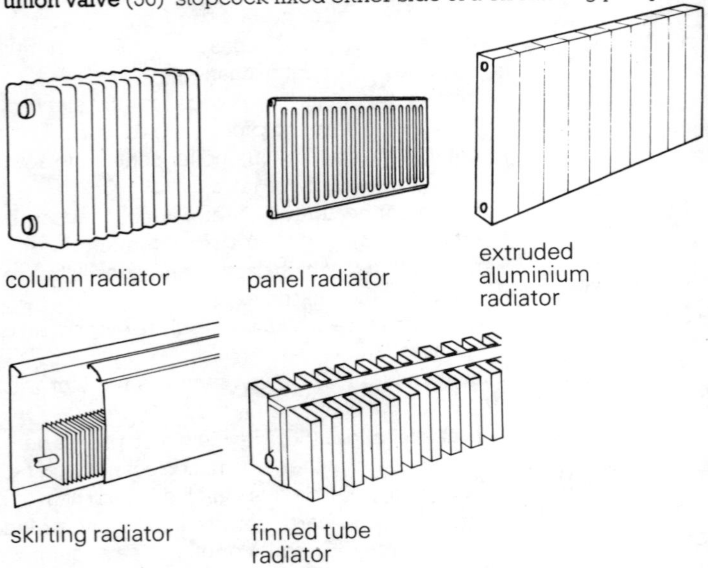

column radiator   panel radiator   extruded aluminium radiator

skirting radiator   finned tube radiator

fig 139 Radiators

8.6.b Actions

adjusting a machine (D7) making small alterations to a machine to make it work better

balancing a heating system (D7) adjusting a boiler and radiators so that all parts of a building are heated properly

bleeding (D7) removing air caught in a hot water heating system

commissioning (D7) testing and adjusting machinery and leaving it in proper working order

installing a heating system (D6) fixing in place all the parts of a heating system

priming a pump (D7) getting a pump started by passing water through it

8.6.c General

boiler capacity (56.1) amount of heat energy that a boiler is able to give out (measured in kW)

ceiling heating (56.3) type of heating which uses electric elements in the ceiling

chimney brick or block flue built into a building

combustion burning; eg fuel combustion takes place inside a boiler

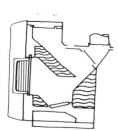

gravity feed boiler

combustion air (56.1) supply of air needed by a boiler so that it can burn fuel

convection current (56) warm air which moves around a room

district heating (56.2) heating system in which many buildings are supplied with hot water from a big boiler house

energy conservation finding ways to use less fuel for heating and other purposes

fuel (5.1) material which may be burned to give heat

gravity feed (56.1) supply of solid fuel to a boiler by dropping from a container (a hopper) as fuel is burned up

heat warmth

hopper (56.1) fuel container in a gravity feed boiler

maintenance period period of several months in which machinery has to be repaired by the firm that installed it

one-pipe system (56.3) see fig. 140

products of combustion (56.1) burnt fuel gases from a boiler which are removed by the flue

radiant heat (56) heat which passes through space, eg the heat from the sun

solar heating (5_) using heat from the sun for space or water heating

space heating (56) the heating of rooms in a building

temperature degree (level) of heat in substance or an object, eg 0°C (freezing point of water) and 100°C (boiling point of water)

two-pipe system (56.3) see fig. 141

under floor heating (56.3) type of heating in which electric elements or hot water pipes are laid in the floor

wet system (56) heating system which uses water to carry heat

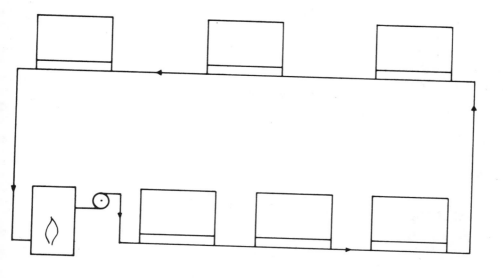

fig 140 One-pipe system of heating pipework

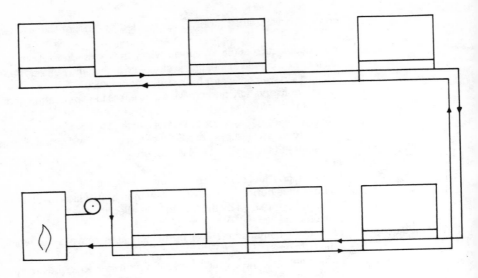

fig 141 Two-pipe system of heating pipework

8.7 Air Conditioning (57)

8.7.a Materials and Components

fan

grilles

air filter (57.5) device which air passes through to be cleaned

air handling unit (57.1) central plant which contains a large fan to pump air round a building

air washer (57.5) device which cleans air using a spray of water

attenuator (68.8) device which reduces the noise passing along an air duct

ceiling diffuser (57) grille through which air passes into a room from a duct above the ceiling

chiller (57.5) device which makes air cold

condenser (57.5) device which removes water from air; the water condenses on to a cold surface

constant flow rate controller device fixed in an air duct to make the air pass through the duct at the right speed

de-humidifier (57.5) device which removes water from air

distribution head (57) ceiling air grille

duct (57) see fig. 142; air ducts are made of galvanised steel sheet, aluminium sheet, or glass reinforced plastic (GRP)

extract fan (57) fan which removes air from a room

fan (57) machine which pumps air

filter see air filter

fire damper (68.5) device which closes up an air duct if a fire starts

grille cover through which air can pass

humidifier (57.5) device which puts moisture (water) into air

intumescent fire damper (68.5) fire damper made of material which gets bigger to close the duct if it gets hot

recuperator (57) device which takes the heat from extract air passing out of a building; this is called heat recovery

refrigeration plant (57.5) machine which makes air cool (cold)

solid absorbent (68.8) solid material fixed inside an air duct to reduce noise in the duct

steel curtain (68.5) type of fire damper, often used with a fusible link; see 5.6

thermal wheel type of recuperator which turns round as the air flows out

water chiller see chiller

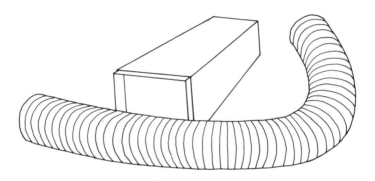

fig 142 Ductwork

7.b General

acoustic lining (68.8) see 8.7.a **solid absorbent**

air change rate (57) the number of times each hour that the air in a room is removed and replaced; eg six air changes per hour

air conditioning (57) control of air flow and temperature in a building by a machine

condensation water vapour in the air changing to water drops on a cold surface such as a window

evaporation the reverse of condensation caused by warming water

extract air (57) air which is removed from a room or building

heat recovery (57) see 8.7.a **recuperator**

humidity measure of the amount of water in the air

moisture water, wetness

natural ventilation (57) movement of air in a room caused by an open window or a grille

noise transmission movement of sound through a structure, duct or pipe

plenum (57) large space in which air is treated (heated or cooled) before being ducted around the building

pressure balance (57) the positive ($+$) or negative ($-$) air pressure in a room caused by the air conditioning

recirculation (57) the re-use (use a second time) of extract air in an air conditioning system

sound absorber (57) device or material which stops noise from passing along a duct

steam injection use of steam (hot water vapour) to make air moist (wet)

steam

supply air (57) air which is pumped into a room or building

trunking ductwork

velocity speed, rate of flow

ventilation (57) circulation of fresh air in a building

vibration tiny movements caused by a machine

8.8 Services Installations

Drawings and Specifications Symbols

Drainage

DP○ discharge pipe
—·—·— drain pipe
FAI☐ fresh air inlet
GT☐ grease trap
G☐ gully
IT☐ intercepting trap
MH☐ manhole (soil)
MH○ manhole (surface water)
☐ rainwater head
RWO ☐ rainwater outlet
RWP○ rainwater pipe
RWS☐ rainwater shoe
RE ɑ CE○ rodding/cleaning eye
VP○ vent pipe

Water supply

◎ calorifier (indirect cylinder)
CWC☐ cold water cistern
CWT☐ cold water storage tank
H & CWT☐ combination tank
DT ⟊ draining tap/cock
GWH☐ gas water heater
F & EXP☐ header feed and expansion tank
HB ⟊ hose bib

⊢ hot/cold water draw off
HWC ○ hot water cylinder
HWT☐ hot water tank
↺ immersion heater
⊕ mixing control valve
SV ⊱ safety valve
⊶ stop valve/cock
WM ⊣○⊢ water meter
⟟ water pump

Gas

⊚ gas meter
G ⊼ gas plug in point
⅝|½ supply pipe, change of size
—⟊— gas cock
⊤ gas point
—⊩— gas valve

Power (electrical)

⊠ cooker control unit
☐ distribution board
○ electricity meter
☐ main control
▷ power point
▷ switch socket outlet
✔ switch
✔ 2-way switch

180

Lighting

- ⟁ discharge lamp
- ○ filament lamp
- ◉ lighting column
- ❦ pull/pendant switch
- ⊦○ wall lamp

Heating

- ᴮ☐ boiler
- ⌑ surface panel ceiling type
- ⊟ convector heater
- ᶜ☐ cooker
- ᶜ/ᴮ☐ cooker boiler
- ☖ electric unit heater
- ♣ unit heater
- ⟺ radiator
- ⊤ thermostat

Ventilation

- ⩗ extract fan
- ᴴ● humidifier
- ⩘ supply fan

Communications

- ♫ bell
- ⊙ bell push
- ⊘ clock
- ▭ control board
- ◎ fire alarm
- △ telephone (internal)
- ▲ telephone (public)
- ᴛᵛ⊤ television socket

Fire fighting

- ⊓ hose cradle/reel
- ▽ fire extinguisher
- ⊕ fire hydrant
- ⓢ sprinkler

Sanitation

- ▭ bath
- ⓤ bidet
- ▦ wash basin
- ⓈⓈ shower unit
- ⌓⌇ urinal
- ⊽ w.c.

9 External Works and Landscaping

Language Practice

9.1.a Paving

'The last-minute rush'
It is often necessary to leave all the external works on site till last, so
that they will not be damaged while other work is being completed.
Sometimes the last jobs have to be hurried in order to be finished on
time.

fig 143

Stanley – *Foreman Pavior*   Paul – *Pavior*   (Peter – *Site
Agent*)   (Sandra – *Paul's wife*)   (Len – *Chief Foreman*)

Stan Morning, Paul. Do you know, Peter's just told me the handover
date for the offices has been brought forward to the end of next
week.

Paul The end of next week? – you're joking. We've got to pave the
whole of the courtyard first, haven't we?

Stan Yes, of course we have. That's just what I came to see you about.
Er – I wondered if you'd mind working evenings next week.

Paul Well, I'm not very keen on working overtime just now, Stan. I
told you Sandra's started working nights at the hospital, didn't I? So
we don't see that much of each other at the moment. She gets really
fed up with being on her own in the evenings.

Stan Oh, go on, Paul, it's only a week, you know. There's no point getting another gang here just for a day or two. It'll be good money for you, too.

Paul Well, I'm sorry, Stan, but I would prefer not to, if you don't mind.

Stan But look here, Paul, it's up to us now to get this job finished on time.

Paul Yes, but a week early? It's too much to ask.

Stan But you know how hard everyone else has had to work to keep on programme.

Paul Hmm.

Stan And we've got a really good set of drawings this time. There won't be any hold-ups on this job, I promise you.

Paul Well, I don't care, I . . .

Stan Look, Paul, we've got full layout drawings here showing where everything is – the falls, the drainage channels, everything. And look at these sections showing all the gradients of the ramps, all the edge details – we've got all we need to know.

Paul Yes, but I . . .

Stan And Len says all the other gangs are busy at the moment, you see. So I told him I thought you'd help out. Please, Paul.

Paul Oh all right, Stan, I'll do it. But I don't know what Sandra's going to say. And I'll tell you this – it'll be the last time you'll get me to do anything I don't want to.

Stan Thanks, Paul.

---

courtyard *see* 9.5.b
damage harm, break
drainage channel *see* fig. 147
external works work on areas outside a building
fall slope, gradient
fed up with tired of
gang *see* 0.1
gradient degree of slope, eg 1:15
handover handing of keys of a finished building to a client

hold-up delay
keen on happy about
layout drawing *see* 0.2
on programme on time with work
overtime extra working hours
pave lay paving slabs; *see* 9.5.a
ramp *see* 9.5.b
section *see* 0.2

Answer the questions.

1 What work do the paviors have to finish before the handover date?
2 What does Stan want Paul to do so they can finish the work on time?
3 Why doesn't Paul see very much of his wife at the moment?
4 Why is Stan sure there won't be any hold-ups on the job?
5 What do the sections show?
6 Why did Stan tell Len that he thought Paul would help out?

Fill in the blanks in this conversation between Len and Stan.

Len Oh, Stan, you know the handover date has been brought forward to the end of next week, don't you?

Stan ....

Len Oh dear, there's quite a bit of work still to do, then, isn't there?

Stan ....

Len No, I'm afraid not. There aren't any other gangs free at the moment, you see.

Stan ....

Len He won't mind a bit of overtime, will he? I should think he'd be glad of the money.

Stan ....

Len Hmm, that doesn't sound too hopeful. Do you think you'll be able to persuade him to do it?

Stan ....

Len Yes. Perhaps he won't mind if he knows there aren't going to be any hold-ups.

9.1.b More uses of '-ing' forms

Here is a short passage about Paul.

Paul isn't very *keen on working* overtime. He is *tired of getting* home late, and *fed up with spending* so long on site every day. But the foreman knows he's *used to doing* it now.

Look at the '-ing' forms that have been used here. Each time they follow an adjective + preposition (on, of, with, etc) phrase. Here are some more adjective + preposition phrases which you might find useful on site. They can all be followed by '-ing' forms too.

> afraid of
> good at/bad at
> interested in
> sure of/certain of
> worried about

Look through the conversation for examples of '-ing' forms used with some of the phrases we have talked about. Now choose an adjective + preposition phrase to complete each of these sentences, and put the verb in brackets ( ) into its '-ing' form.

Example:
Paul isn't very . . . . . (tell) Sandra he's on overtime next week.
Paul isn't very *keen on telling* Sandra he's on overtime next week.

---

1 Stanley is . . . . . (finish) the job behind schedule.

2 Paul is very . . . . . (work) to a deadline, because he works well under pressure.

3 The paving is always one of the last jobs, so Stanley is . . . . . (do) his work in a hurry.

4 They would be . . . . . (complete) the paving on time if Paul agreed to the overtime.

5 Paul says he's . . . . . (stay) late on site because he doesn't see much of Sandra.

6 Stanley is . . . . . Paul (say) he's not going to do it.

Remember that these adjective + preposition phrases are not always followed by '-ing' forms. The can be followed by nouns too.

> He is *interested in his work.*
> Stanley is *sure of a good result.*
> Paul is *fed up with overtime.*

9.2.a Landscaping

'Fair weather, foul weather'

Sowing seed and planting trees and shrubs can only be carried out at the right time of year. Landscape work is therefore difficult to fit into a building programme.

fig 144

Peter – *Site Agent*   Sylvia – *Landscape Architect*

Sylvia Oh, hello, Peter. I've just brought these final landscape drawings over. How are you getting on with things?

Peter Oh, not as well as I'd hoped, I'm afraid. You know the grass sowing was programmed for the end of the sowing season? Well, there's just no way we'll be ready by then.

Sylvia Yes, it's been such awful weather, hasn't it? What we could do with now is a good dry spell, or the ground will be too wet even to prepare for any sowing.

Peter It really has been wet this autumn. And do you know, since last winter we've lost about six weeks' working time through inclement weather. And this is supposed to be the better part of the year! It's really put us back.

Sylvia I'm sure it has. And of course we could be into the cold weather again before we know it. Goodness knows how many weeks' work will be lost once winter really sets in.

Peter Hmm. That's just what worries me. But anyway, we do expect to finish the external works by Christmas, and then the landscape contractor will be able to make a start, all being well.

Sylvia Well, we could be lucky, I suppose. If there's no freezing we might be able to plant trees. But the rest of the plant material . . . well, we'll just have to hope for more favourable conditions in the spring.

all being well if everything goes well
dry spell period of dry weather
external works work on areas outside a building
favourable good, helpful

foul bad
freezing temperatures of 0°C and below
inclement weather bad weather
plant *see* 9.6.a *and* 9.6.c

programme *see* 0.2

put **back** delay

seed *see* 9.6.a

set in get established

shrub *see* 9.6.a

sow *see* 9.6.c

sowing season time of year
  when sowing may be done

worry be concerned

Answer the questions.

1 When was Peter hoping to get the grass sowing done?

2 Why haven't they been able to keep on programme with the
landscape work?

3 How much working time have they lost since last winter? Is that
usual for the better half of the year?

4 Do they expect to lose any working time during the winter?

5 When will the landscape contractor be able to start?

6 When will they begin planting?

**Peter is telling Sid, the clerk of works, about how work is going. Fill in
the blanks.**

Sylvia .... this morning and I told her
.... She said if we didn't have a dry spell
soon .... Do you know, over the last six
months or so .... , and now winter's on the
way again. Anyway, we're pretty sure we'll ....
.... by Christmas. But I don't suppose we'll
be able to plant any trees, unless of course ....
....

**9.2.b Talking about
weather**

Weather conditions are important on a building site because they
have a great effect on whether work can go on as planned. Here are
some of the weather expressions you can find in the conversation.
Look and see how they are used.

  awful weather

  inclement weather

  winter sets in

  freezing

  a good dry spell

  more favourable conditions

Usually it is impossible to carry on working without cover in high
winds, sub-zero temperatures, heavy rainfall and extremely hot
weather. Look at these pictures of different weather conditions on
site. (A list of the different weather conditions is given at the end of
the exercise – in the wrong order). Describe the weather conditions
for each picture, and say whether you think the men will be able to
carry out the planned job, explaining why or why not.

Example:

Planting trees (very windy)

It is very windy today. The men will not be able to plant trees
because young trees might be damaged or blown over in high winds.

1 Laying paving slabs

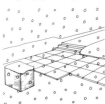

4 Planting out seedlings

2 Sowing grass seed

5 Building planting boxes

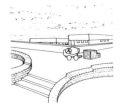

3 Asphalting an access road

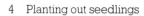

6 Excavating a pool

Weather conditions.

torrential rain
hot and dry
freezing

favourable conditions
light rain
snowing

3.a Roads and Footpaths

'Falls on a Footpath'

A drawing does not often show every piece of information which is needed to do a job of work properly. In building, it is usually easy for the designer and the workman to discuss the job.

fig 145

Len – *Chief Foreman*   John – *Civil Engineer*

Len Would you mind coming into the office a moment, John? We might as well make use of you while you're here! There's somethin I'd just like to ask you about.

John Sure.

(*inside the office*)

John Now, what can I do for you?

Len Well, we're setting out the footpaths now. We're trying to get th path edgings in first so the mains services can be laid in between. You know there's supposed to be a camber on this path, don't you – that's what these drawings show, anyway.

John Yes, that's right. So you'll be setting the two edgings at the sam level, then.

Len Well, yes . . . only now we've got to this landscaped area. There are some brick planting boxes down one side of the path, if you remember – here on the drawing, look.

John Right. So you'll have to change from a camber to a crossfall, there, won't you?

Len Yes, that's no problem, of course. But what do you want betwee the planting boxes?

John Let's just see . . . well, I suppose it would be better to change back to a camber, wouldn't it? But I see your point. It'll look rather odd, if you do that – especially looking along it from this position.

Len Yes, I'm sure it will. No, my feeling is that we'll have to lay it to a crossfall right up as far as the car park. What do you think?

John Yes, I think you're right.

Len Okay. Oh, while I think of it, could you just come outside and loc at the gulley pots that were delivered yesterday? I'm not sure they've brought the right size.

camber *see* 9.5.b
crossfall *see* 9.5.b
edging *see* 9.5.a
footpath *see* 9.5.b
gulley pot *see* 9.5.a **gulley**
level height

mains services gas, water or electricity supply pipes or cables
odd strange, peculiar
planting box raised container for plants

Answer the questions.

1 Why does Len ask John to go into the office?

2 How should the surface of the path be laid, according to the drawings?

3 Where are the brick planting boxes?

4 How will they lay the path beside the planting boxes?

5 Why can't they change back to a camber between the planting boxes?

6 How far will they have to lay the path to a crossfall?

Complete the sentences.

1 The mains services have to be laid . . . . . .

2 There is a camber on the path, so . . . . . .

3 In the landscaped area the path will be laid to a crossfall because . . . . . .

4 It would look rather odd if . . . . . between the planting boxes.

5 The path will look best if . . . . . .

6 Len asks the civil engineer to check over the gulley pots because . . . . . .

.b Prepositions
place

Look at these expressions from the conversation:

into the office   *at* the same level

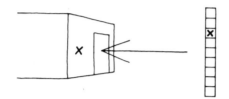

down one side   *on* the drawing

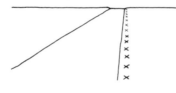 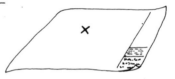

between the planting boxes   looking *along* it

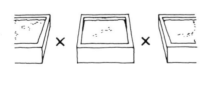 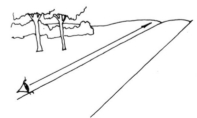

as far as the car park

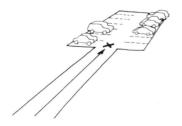

189

All these expressions use prepositions of place or *Where?* prepositions (in *italics*). These prepositions are of course very important on site. Practise using them in this exercise by choosing th correct prepositions to fill in the blanks.

Example:
Len shows John the paths . . . . . his drawing . . . . . the office.
Len shows John the paths on his drawing in the office.

---

1 John is standing . . . . . the office when Len asks him to come . . . .

2 Water will not collect . . . . . the path if the surface is laid to a camber or a crossfall.

3 There are planting boxes . . . . . the side of the path and a car par . . . . . the end.

4 There will be planting boxes . . . . . the path and they are going t plant shrubs . . . . . them.

5 John doesn't want the path to change from a crossfall back to a camber . . . . . the planting boxes because it will look odd.

6 John and Len walk . . . . . the car park area to get a better idea of what the grounds will be like . . . . . the building.

Communication on Site

Making requests, agreeing/refusing, and persuading

9.4.a Requests

A request is usually a polite form of command. Instead of telling someone to do something, we ask whether they are willing or able do it. Look at these examples of requests. Instead of saying 'Go and get me that report' we might say:

Will/would you (please) go and get me that report?
Can/could you (possibly) go and get me that report?

Practise making these commands into requests, using a different fo each time.

1 Fetch me a spade when you go to the store.

2 Tell the foreman the ground's too wet for sowing.

3 Check which side of the path the planting boxes will be.

4 Come down and help me with the footpath layout when you've finished up here.

5 Don't leave tools lying around in the lunch break.

6 Get on with the paving as fast as you can.

9.4.b Polite requests

The form of request we use may depend on who we are talking to (see 1.4.b: job rank). To people of high job rank we are likely to choose politer forms of request. We may also use politer forms whe the thing we are requesting is difficult or unpleasant or requires a l of effort. Here are some politer forms of request:

Do you think you could get me that report?
Would you mind getting me that report?
I wonder if you'd mind getting me that report?
Would it be possible for you to get me that report?
I wonder if you could possibly get me that report?

190

Now practise requesting the same things as before, this time using the politer request forms instead.

9.4.c Agreeing/ Refusing

When we request someone to do something, rather than commanding him, we give him the opportunity of agreeing or refusing to do it. Some things he might say in agreement are:

Yes, of course.
With pleasure.
Sure.
Certainly.
Okay.
All right.

But if he's not keen on doing it, or can't, he might refuse like this:

Well, I'd rather not, if you don't mind.
I'm sorry, I'm afraid not.
I'm afraid I can't (just now).
I can't manage it (at the moment).

When we refuse a request we often like to give a reason (see 3.4.a). Look back to conversation 9.1.a. What reason does Paul give for not wanting to work overtime?

Now try this exercise. Write short conversations to practise first agreeing to a request and then refusing. Think up a suitable reason to give each time someone refuses. Use any form of request that seems suitable.

Example:

Paul Find out when the handover date is. (Stan)
Paul Do you think you could find out when the handover date is, Stan?
Stan (*Agreeing*) Yes, of course.
   (*Refusing*) I'm afraid I can't at the moment, Paul. It's not been decided yet.

---

1 Stan Work overtime on Thursday and Friday. (Paul)
2 Peter Bring me the final landscape drawings. (Sylvia)
3 Sylvia Try and get the external works finished by Christmas. (Peter)
4 Len Give me some advice about these footpaths. (John)
5 Peter Come and have a look at the brick planting boxes if you've got time. (Sylvia)
6 Paul Give me a hand with these paving slabs. (Stan)

9.4.d Persuasion

When someone refuses to do something we have requested, we might have to try a little persuasion. Look back to conversation 9.1.a where Stan is trying to persuade Paul to work overtime. Notice how he tells Paul the good things about doing the work, and tries to show him he is the only person who can do it.

Practise using persuasion in this conversation.

Words you will need:

access road vehicle road leading to buildings
base course *see* 9.5.b
maintenance general repair work
wearing course *see* 9.5.b

Norman, the architect, has specified a 15 mm wearing course and a 30 mm base course on the access road. Peter, the site agent, asks him to make it instead 25 mm and 40 mm thicknesses. When Norman refuses because of the extra cost, Peter tries to persuade him by pointing out that the thicker surface will wear much better and that it will last much longer before needing any maintenance. Write the conversation between them, beginning like this:

Peter *I've been thinking about the surface on this access road, Norman.*

Reference Section

9.5 Hard Landscape (90)

9.5.a Materials and Components

asphalt s5 bituminous material used on the surface of roads

bitumen emulsion s1 liquid containing bitumen, which is brushed or sprayed on to surfaces in road construction

channel (90.4) see fig. 147

clinker Cp3 type of hard ash from a furnace, which is used as hardcore for roads and footpaths

cobbles (90.4) small round stones which are set into the ground in concrete

drainage channel see fig. 147

edging (90.4) material used at the edge of a footpath or paved area; see fig. 147

fence (90.3) see fig. 146 for various types

fire hydrant (90.5) place set in the ground at which water hoses may be connected if there is a fire

fire path pot (90.4) see fig. 147

gravel (90.4)C small stones, sometimes used on the surface of paths

gulley (or gully) (90.5) outlet for storm water in a road

hardcore Cp hard material used as a base for roads, eg crushed stone, crushed concrete

hoggin Cp1 mixture of sand and gravel used in footpath construction

hot rolled asphalt (90.4)s5 asphalt road surface which has to be hot when it is laid

kerbstone (90.4) long piece of stone or concrete used at the edge of a road; see fig. 147

macadam s5 road surface material made from small stones mixed with tar or bitumen

manhole cover (90.4) top or lid of a manhole

paving slab (90.4) flat piece of stone or concrete used for footpaths and paved areas; see fig. 147

paver (90.4) small brick, concrete or stone block used to form a hard, flat surface; see fig. 147

sett (90.4)e small stone block used like a paver; see fig. 147

tar s1 black, sticky material produced from coal

tree grille (90.4) metal grid placed around a tree within a paved area

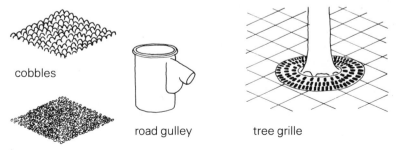

cobbles

gravel

road gulley

tree grille

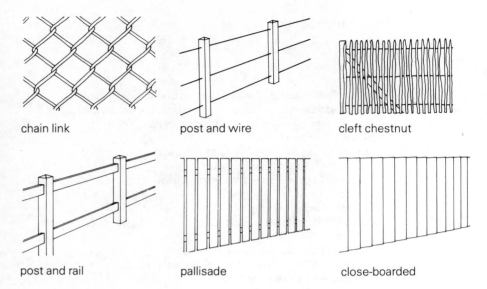

chain link   post and wire   cleft chestnut

post and rail   pallisade   close-boarded

fig 146 Fences

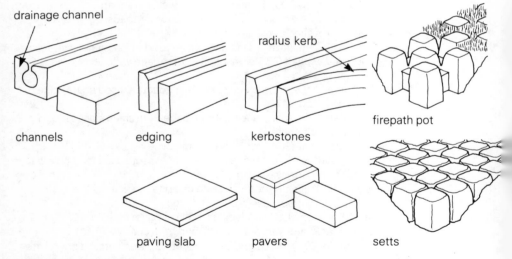

drainage channel

radius kerb

firepath pot

channels   edging   kerbstones

paving slab   pavers   setts

fig 147 Concrete components

9.5.b General   **access** way to get into a place or building
anti-slip surface (90.4) rough surface on a footpath which is not slippery when wet
base (90.4) part of a road laid on top of the sub-base; see fig. 148
base course (90.4) layer of material in road construction; see fig. 148
carriageway (90.4) part of a road used by vehicles
camber (90.4) the falls across a road which allow water to drain away; see fig. 148
courtyard 998 rectangular (▭) space enclosed by buildings

crossfall (90.4) a fall across a road in one direction; see fig. 148

cul-de-sac (90.4) a road which can only be entered at one end; see fig. 151

dropped kerb (90.4) low kerb

dwarf wall (90.3) very low wall

embankment (90.4) bank of earth, eg for a raised footpath

footpath (90.4) route for people walking

footway (90.4) footpath

formation level (90.4) the level of the firm ground upon which a road is built after excavation; see fig. 148

hammer head (90.4) kind of turning head; see fig. 151

kerb (90.4) raised edge of a road; see fig. 148

patio 998 small paved area, often enclosed by a building

pavement (90.4) footpath at the side of a road; see fig. 148

pedestrian person walking

ramp (90.4) footpath which slopes to change its level

revetment (90.4) wall or bank formed with concrete units which retain (hold back) earth

road (90.4) route for vehicles, which may have one or two pavements

road roller (B2i) see fig. 149

screen (90.3) fence or wall which closes off a view, often to make a space more private; plants may also form a screen

service road (90.4) road used only for access to a car park, or for vehicles making deliveries

square 998 rectangular (☐) enclosed area but bigger than a courtyard

stepped ramp (90.4) ramp with steps in it

stepping stone (90.4) stone set within a pool of water

step (90.4) change of level in a footpath

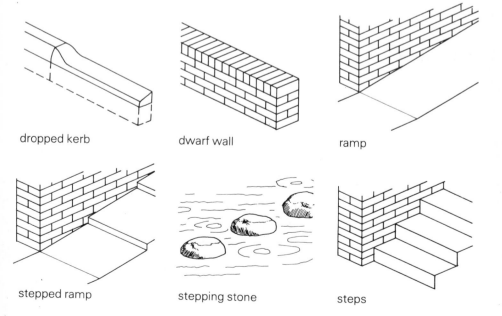

dropped kerb dwarf wall ramp

stepped ramp stepping stone steps

street furniture (90.7) objects fixed outside buildings, eg signs, light columns, seats, litter bins; see fig. 150

sub-base (90.4) part of a road which is laid upon the sub-grade; see fig. 148

sub-grade (90.4) the earth below the formation level on which a road is built; see fig. 148

subway (90.4) footpath which passes under a road

trim (90.4) edging

turning head (90.4) space for vehicles to turn round in; see fig. 151

vehicle means of transport, usually with an engine, eg car, lorry, bus

wearing course (90.4) top layer of material laid on a road; see fig. 148

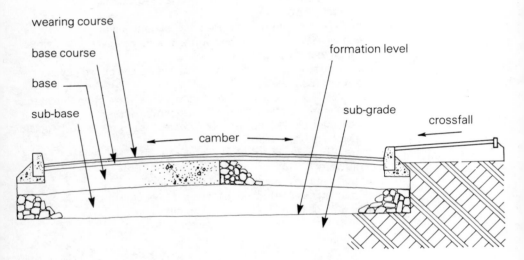

wearing course

base course

base

sub-base

camber

formation level

sub-grade

crossfall

fig 148 Road construction

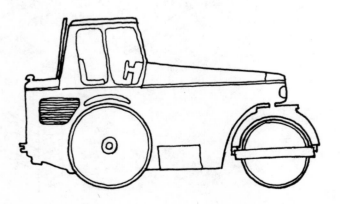

fig 149 Road roller

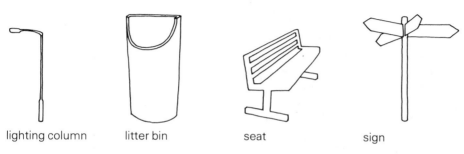

| lighting column | litter bin | seat | sign |

fig 150 Street furniture

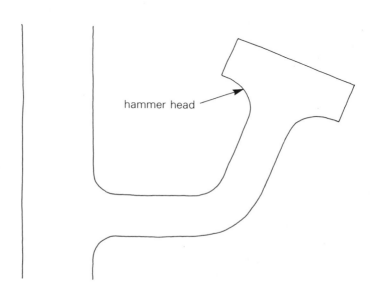

hammer head

fig 151 Plan of a turning head in a cul-de-sac

9.6 Soft Landscape (90)W

9.6.a Plant, Material and Accessories

container-grown plant

bonemeal fertiliser made from animal bones
bush large woody plant; see fig. 152
climbing plant plant which grows up a wall or trellis
compost fertiliser made of rotted plant material
container grown plant plant grown in a pot
deadmen pieces of wood used in guying; see fig. 155
fertiliser material added to soil to feed plants
grass hardy plant with green leaf blades, much used in planting schemes
ground cover plant low plant which spreads across the ground
herbaceous plant plant with soft stems and leaves
hoof and horn fertiliser fertiliser made from horns and feet of animals

seedling

stake

loam rich, soft soil
manure fertiliser which is mostly animal droppings, especially from cows and horses
nitrogen chemical (formula N) which plants need to grow properly
peat soft, dark, fibrous earth used as a form of compost
perennial plant which stays alive for many years
plant living being such as a flowering herb, shrub or bush
potassium chemical (formula K) needed by plants to grow properly
seed tiny thing from which a plant grows
seedling young plant which has just grown from a seed
shrub bush, often flowering
soil see fig. 153
stake wooden post used to support a young tree
subsoil soil below the topsoil; see fig. 8
topsoil top layer of soil in which plants will grow; see fig. 8
tree see fig. 152
tree tie soft strap to fix a tree to a stake
turf piece of grass cut from the ground
weed unwanted wild plant which needs to be removed from a planted area

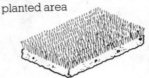

piece of turf

herbaceous plant

bush

deciduous tree

coniferous tree

fig 152 Plants and trees

light sandy soil   medium loam   heavy clay soil

fig 153 Types of soil

bulldozer (B2g) see fig. 6
chain saw (B5) see fig. 154
disc plough (B2) see fig. 154
dragline (B2j) see fig. 6
excavator (B2j) see fig. 6
fork (B7) hand tool for working earth
grader(B2i) machine which finishes off excavated ground to the
    required levels
harrow (B2) see fig. 154
mower (B8) machine for cutting grass
rake (B7) hand tool for working soil
roller (B6f) see fig. 154
rotary cultivator or **rotavator** (B2) see fig. 154
secateurs (pair of) (B7) hand tool for pruning
scraper (B2h) machine for reducing ground levels over large areas
shovel (B7) hand tool for moving earth
spade (B7) hand tool for digging
transplanter (B8p) machine which digs up a tree with the soil around
    the roots; see fig. 154

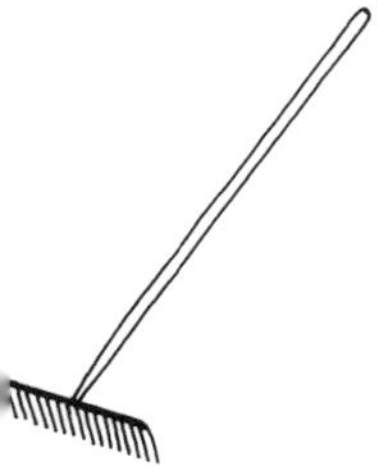

fork

ake 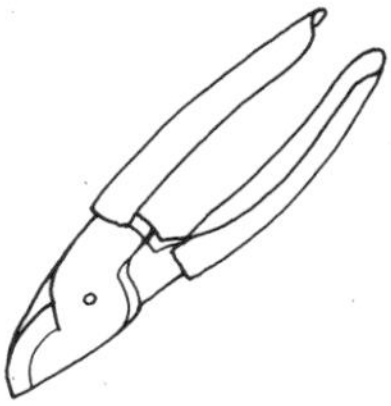
pair of secateurs 
shovel 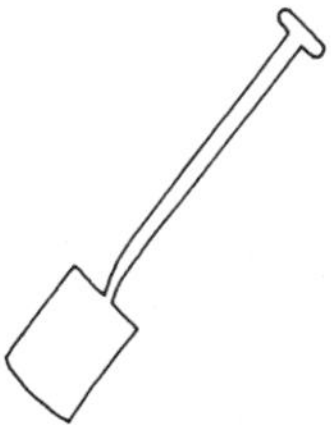
spade

chain saw 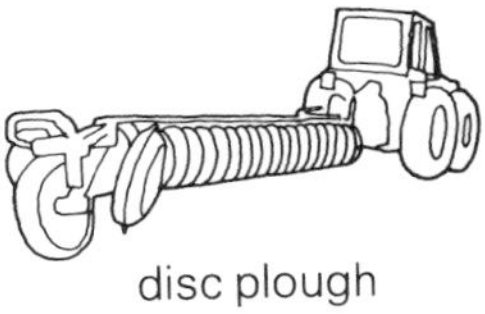
disc plough 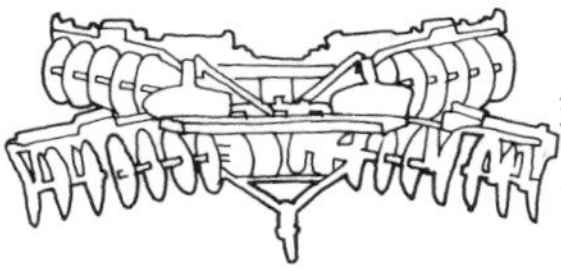
harrow 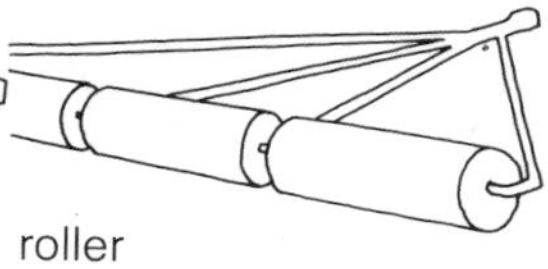
roller

rotary cultivator 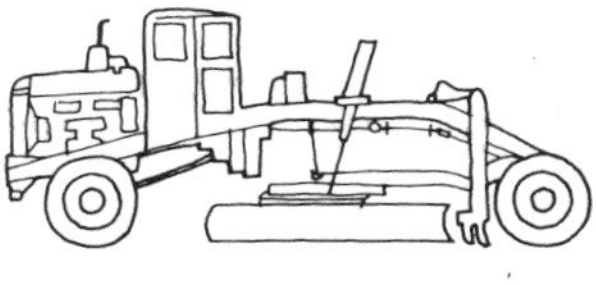
grader

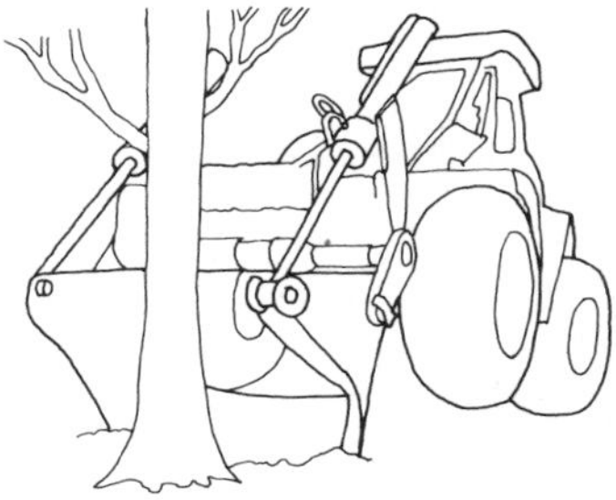

transplanter

fig 154 Landscaping tools

cutting (D2) excavating

dewatering (D2) draining away water when exavating below the water table

digging (D2) removing earth by hand with a spade, or with a machine

establishing getting plants growing properly in a new place

felling (D2) cutting down a tree

firming pressing soil around the roots of a plant or tree

gapping up replacing plants which have died

grading shaping ground to the right levels

guying holding down trees using ropes and stakes; see fig. 155

hydra seeding method of blowing seeds on to steep banks and then mulching them; see fig. 156

lopping cutting branches from a tree

mowing grass cutting grass with a machine

mulching laying material (eg compost) on the ground surface to keep the soil moist (wet)

planting putting a plant or tree into the ground

pruning removing parts of a shrub or tree to improve its shape, or to make it grow new wood

root bracing fixing the roots of a tree into the ground; see fig. 155

seeding sowing seeds

sowing seeds spreading seeds over the ground

stripping (D2) removing the topsoil from a site

topping lightly mowing new grass for the first time

turfing laying turf

underplanting planting ground cover plants under trees or shrubs

watering giving plants water

weeding removing weeds from a planted area

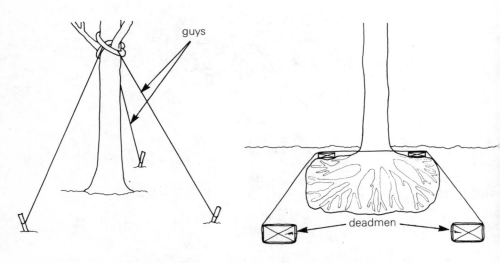

guys

deadmen

fig 155 Guyed tree   **Braced tree**

fig 156 Hydra seeding

6.d *General*

bank steeply sloping surface which often has grass growing on it
branch part of a tree; see fig. 157
containerised grown in a pot
edging (90.4) material used at the edge of a planted area
foliage leaves
ha-ha wall or fence hidden in a ditch; see fig. 158
half-standard tree see fig. 157
hardy able to grow well in a certain climate, ie in certain weather conditions
hedge plants grown in a line to form a screen
hedge bank see fig. 158
irrigation provision of a water supply for plants
land drain (90.5) drain pipes laid to take away water from the ground
landscape the form, shape and features of land
lawn area of grass which is kept well cut
leaf part of a tree; see fig. 157
mound small area of raised ground
nursery place where trees and plants are grown for sale
nursery stock plant or tree which is available at a nursery; ie the nursery has it in stock
park landscaped open space used for leisure

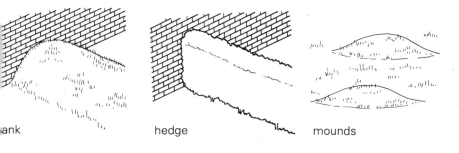

ank   hedge   mounds

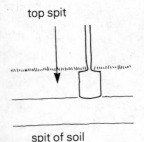

top spit

spit of soil

windbreak

pergola see fig. 158
pitch area on which a game is played, eg football pitch, cricket pitch
planting season time of year at which seeds may be sown or plants and trees may be planted
pond small pool
pool small area of water
root part of a tree in the ground; see fig. 157
root ball roots of a tree with the soil around them
spit spade-depth of soil
spread width of a tree; see fig. 157
stem part of a plant; see fig. 157
standard tree see fig. 157
tilth condition of soil with regard to the size of the lumps of soil; eg a fine tilth (soil well broken up)
tree pit large hole into which a tree is planted
tree surgery tree work which improves the health of a tree
tree work jobs done on a tree; eg pruning
trunk part of a tree; see fig. 157
vegetation plants and trees (collective word)
water table level of water below the ground
windbreak trees planted to shelter an area from the wind.

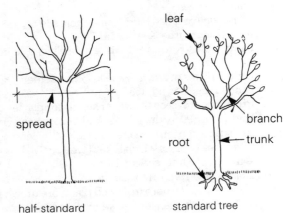

spread

half-standard

leaf

branch

root

trunk

standard tree

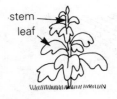

stem

leaf

plant

fig 157 Trees and plants

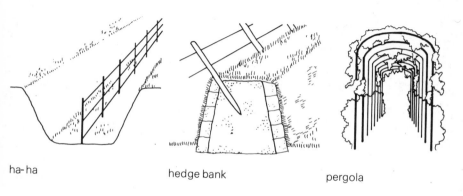

ha-ha

hedge bank

pergola

fig 158 Landscape features